zendoodle coloring

Furry Friends

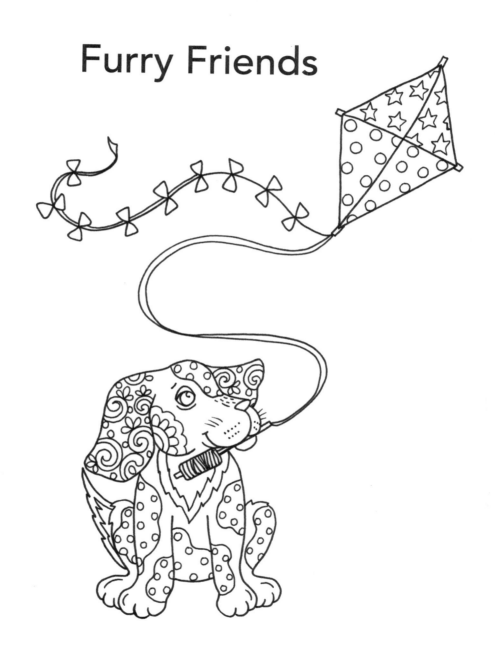

Other great books in the series
zendoodle coloring

zendoodle coloring

Furry Friends

Cuddly Cats and Dogs to Color and Display

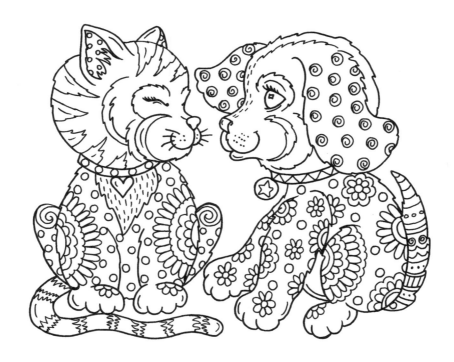

illustrations by

Deborah Muller

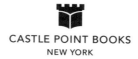

CASTLE POINT BOOKS
NEW YORK

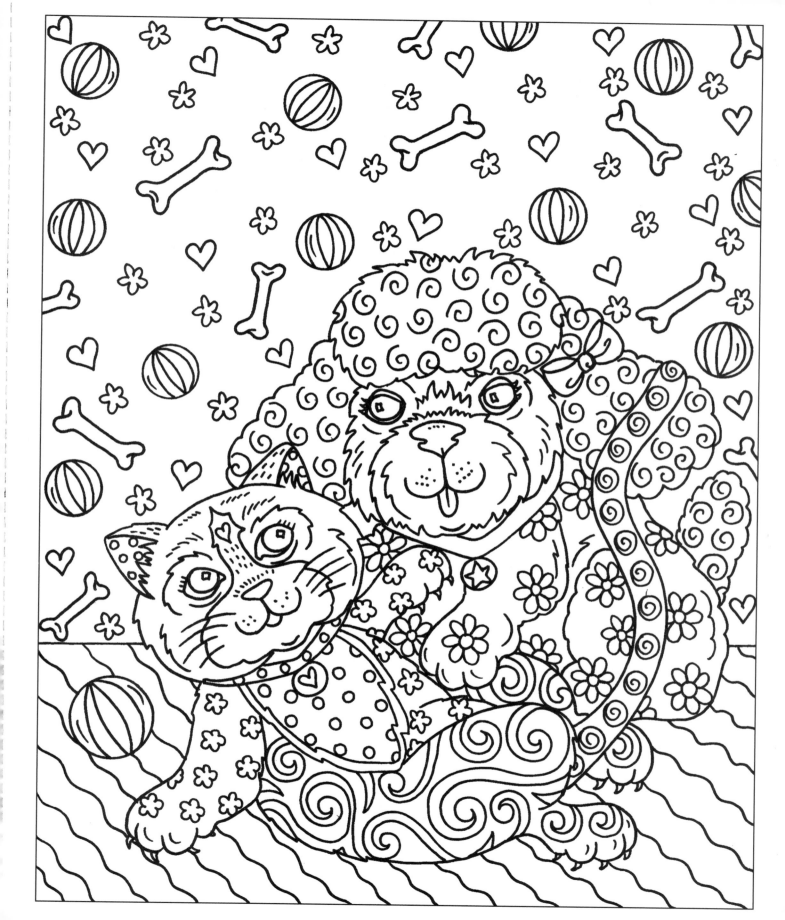

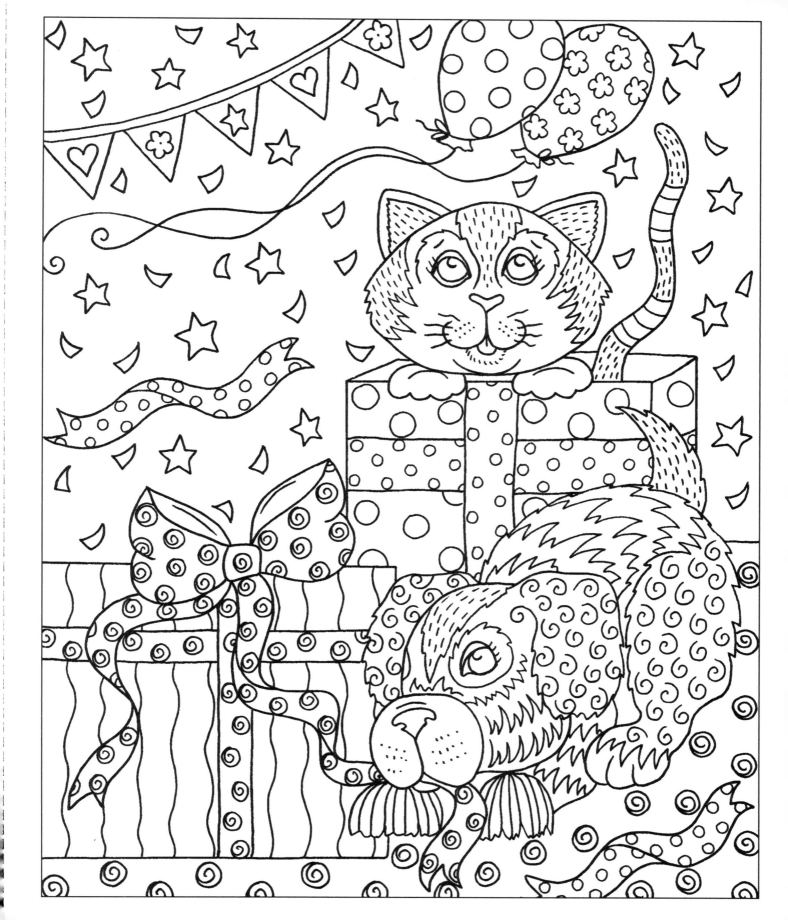

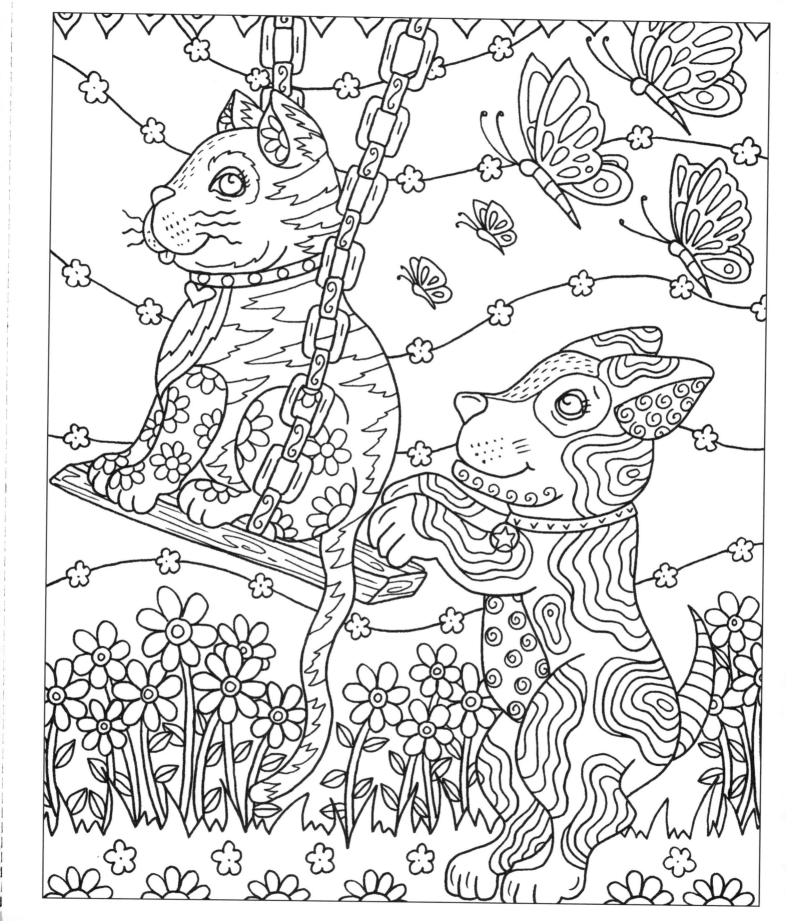

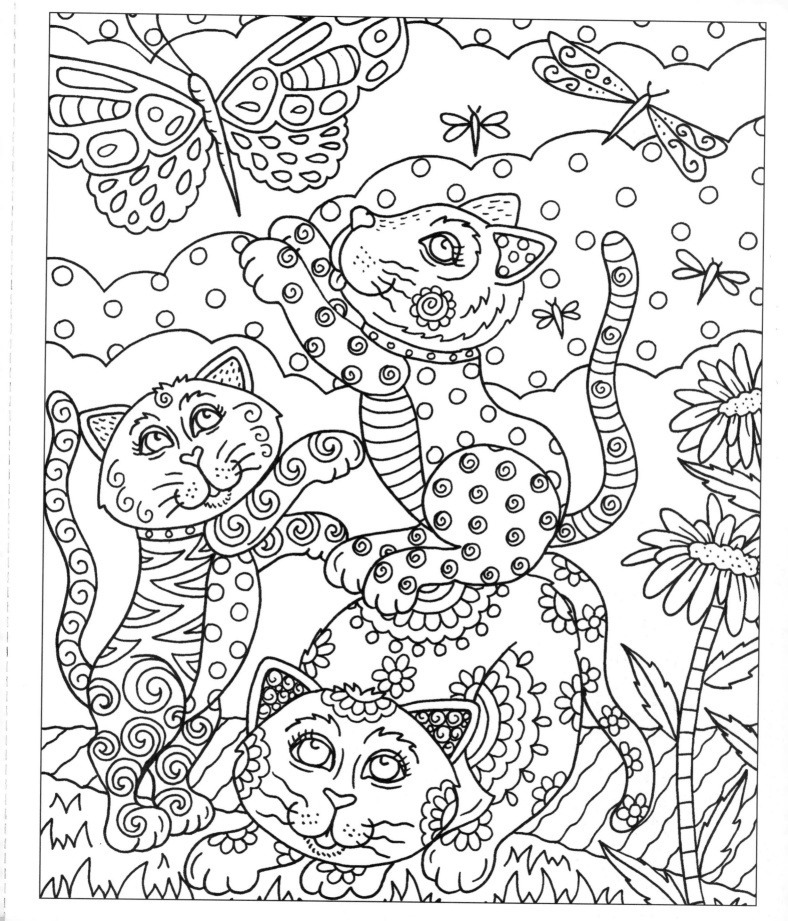

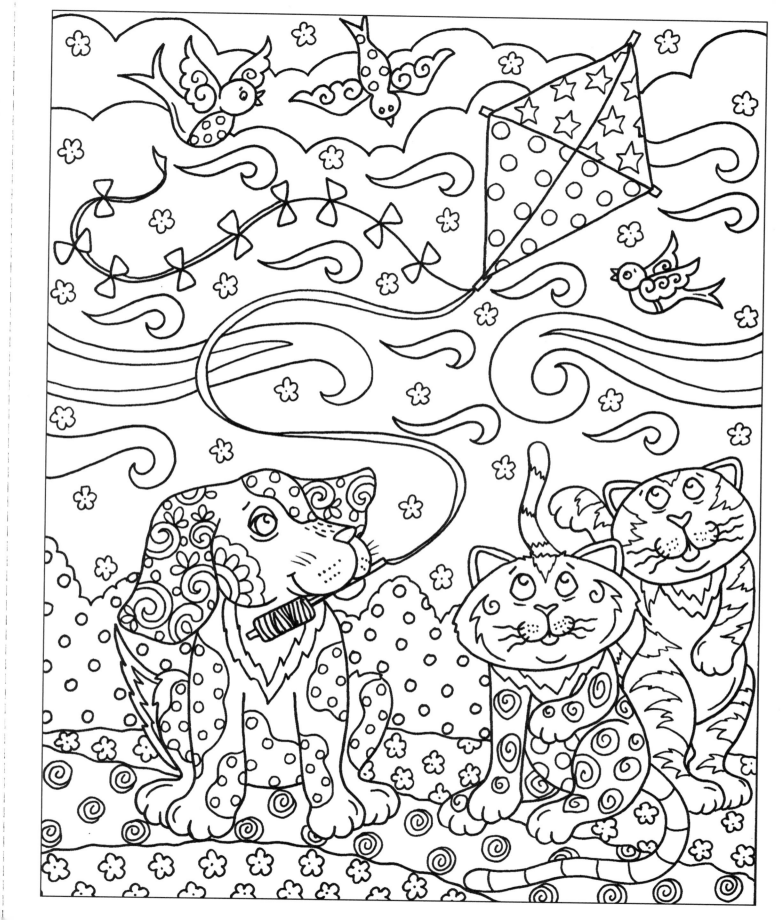

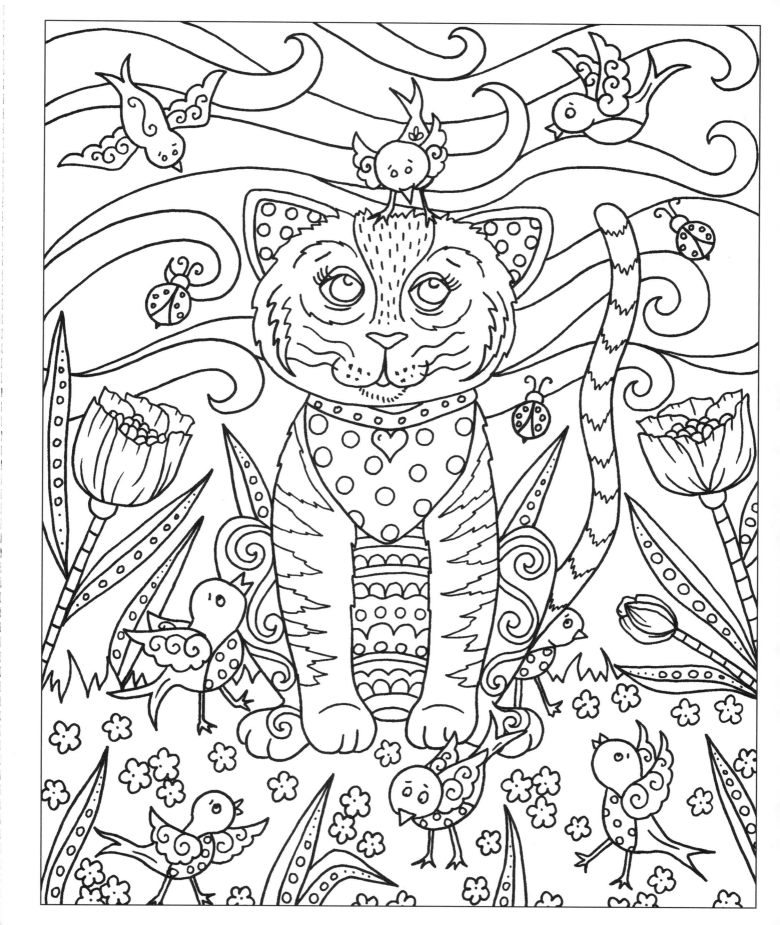

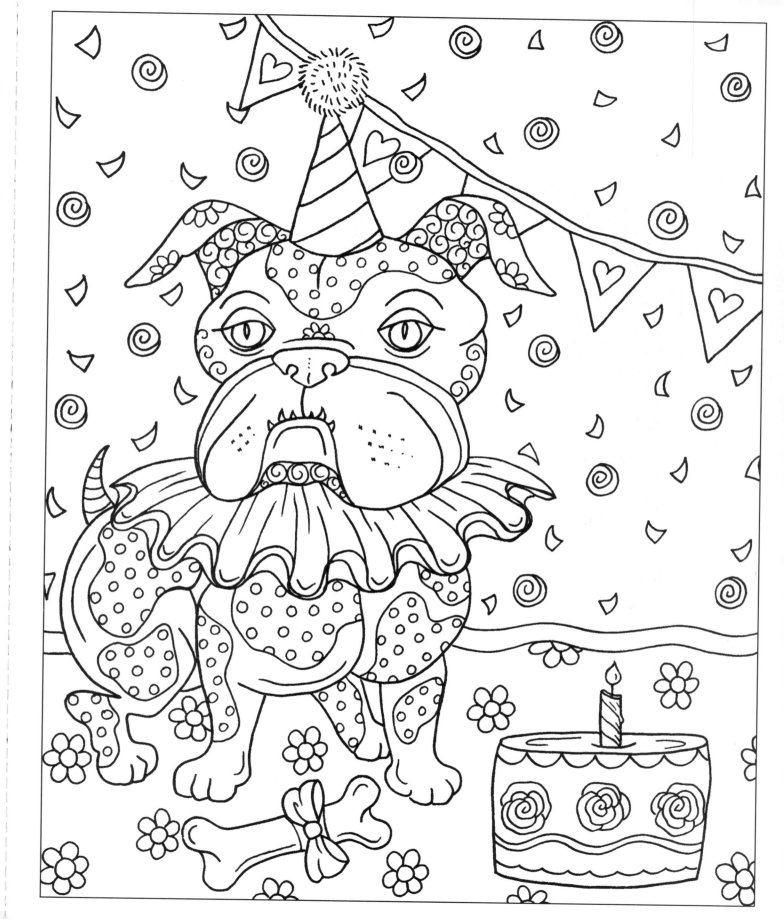

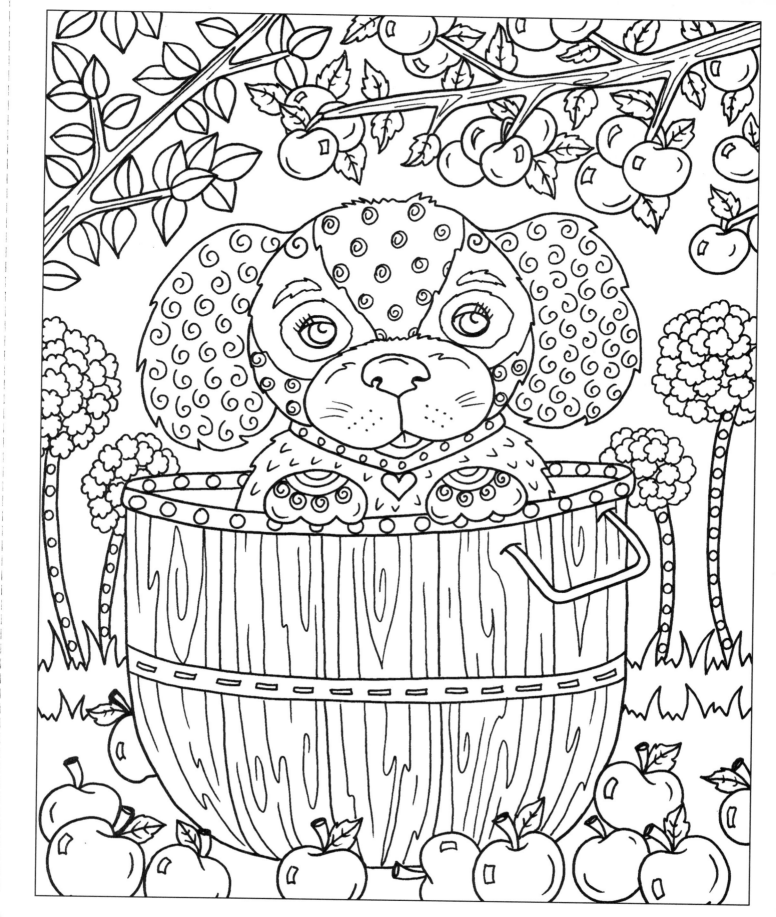

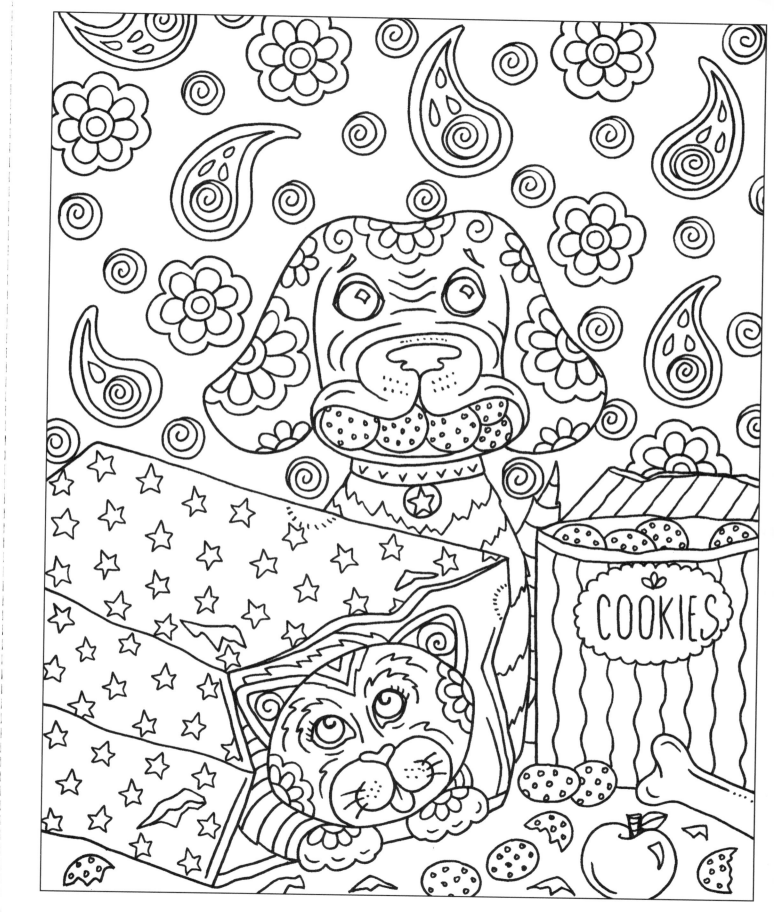

COOKIES

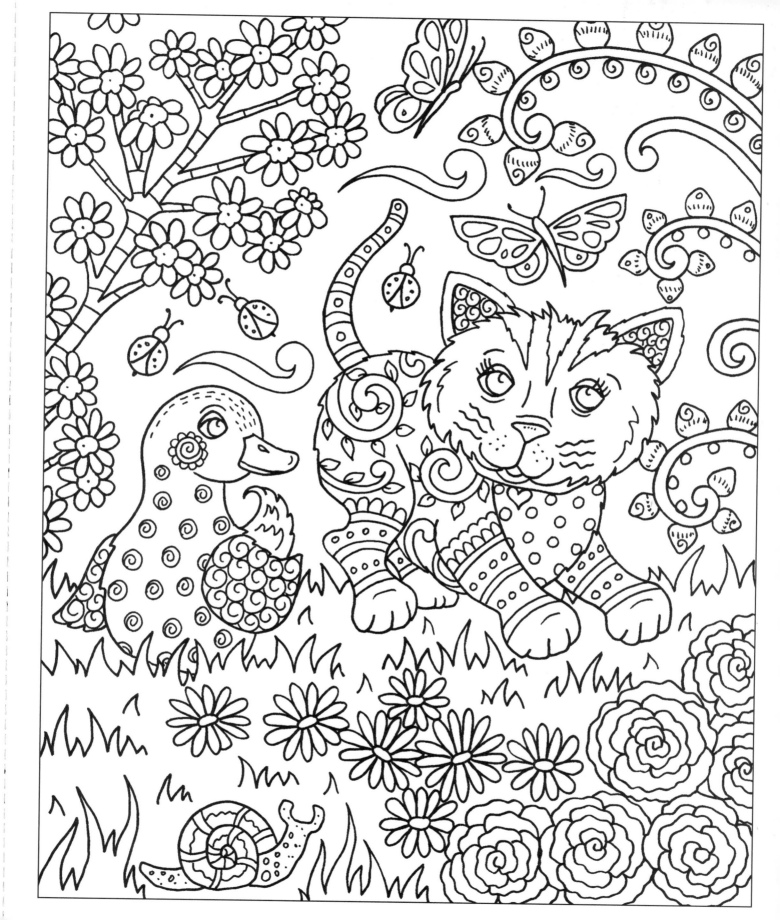

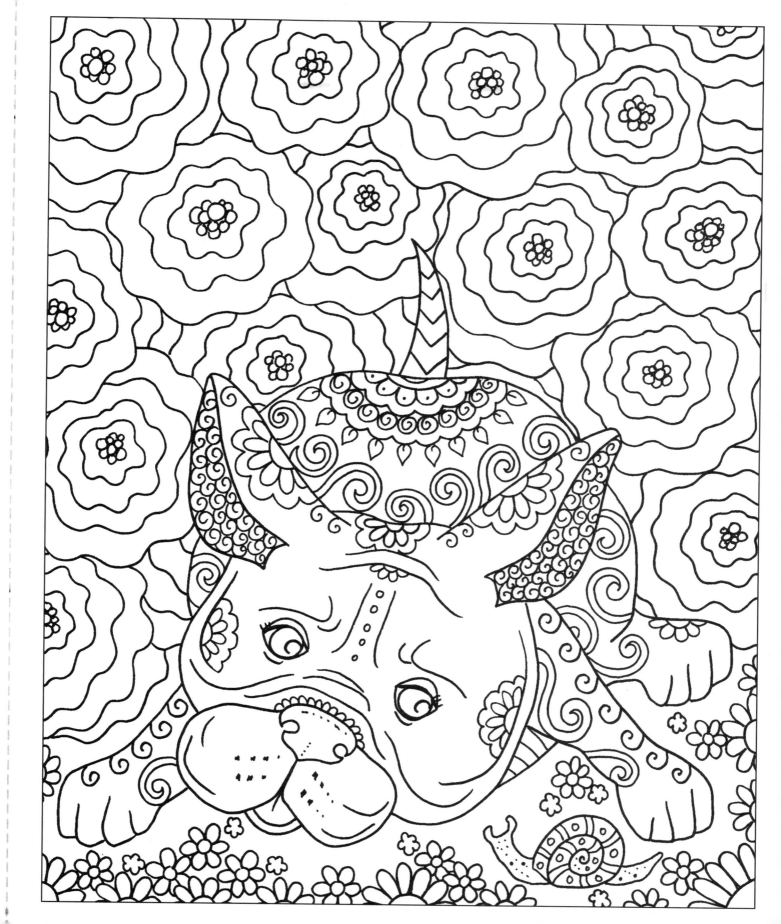

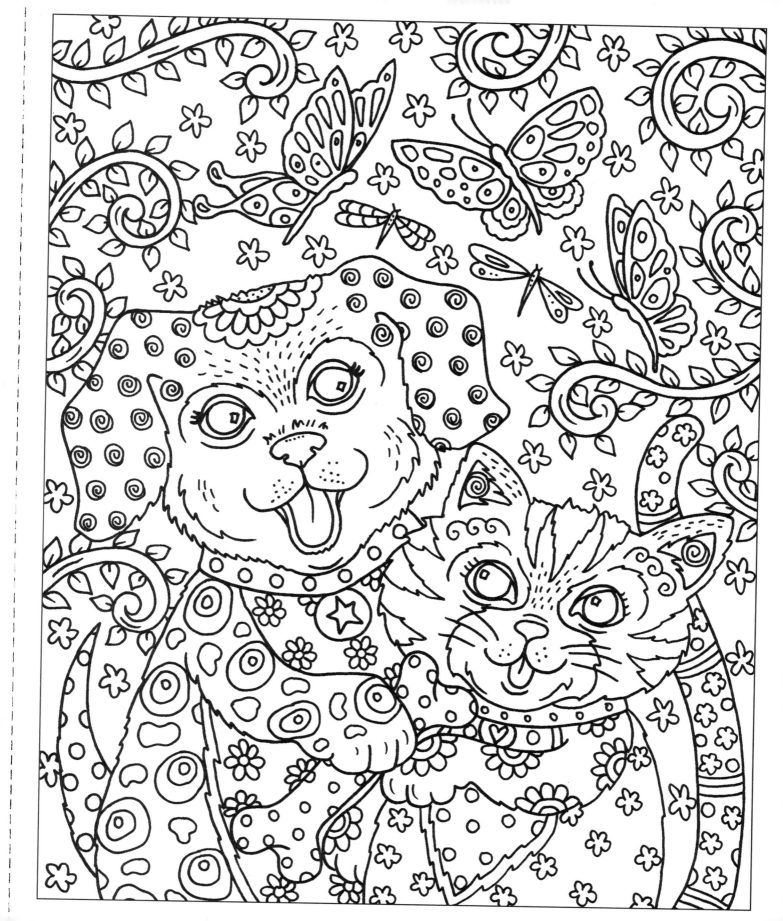

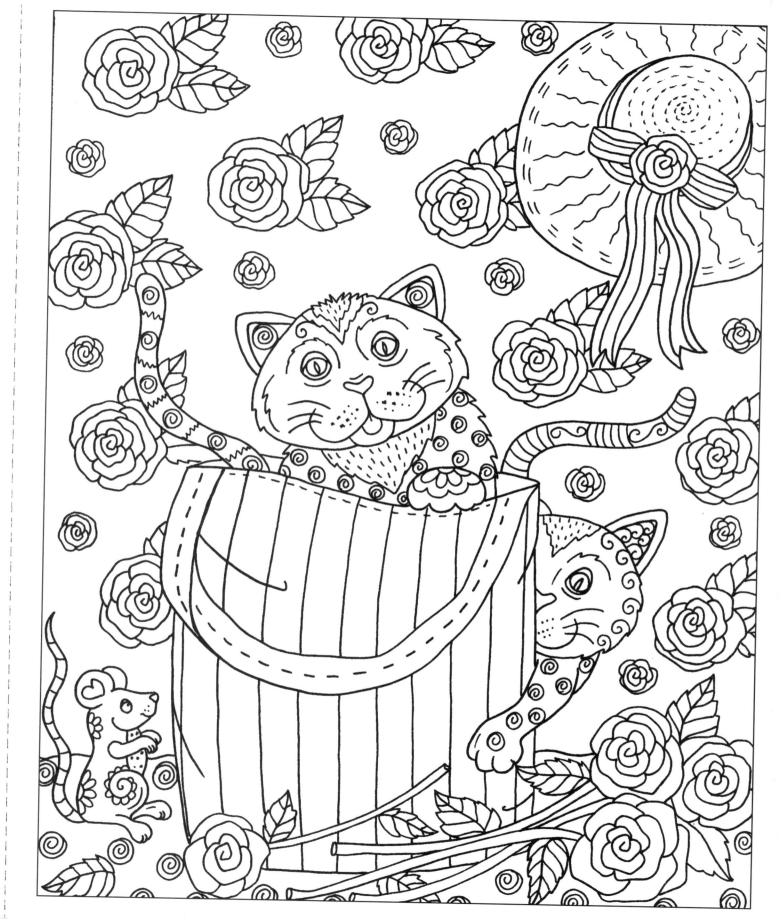

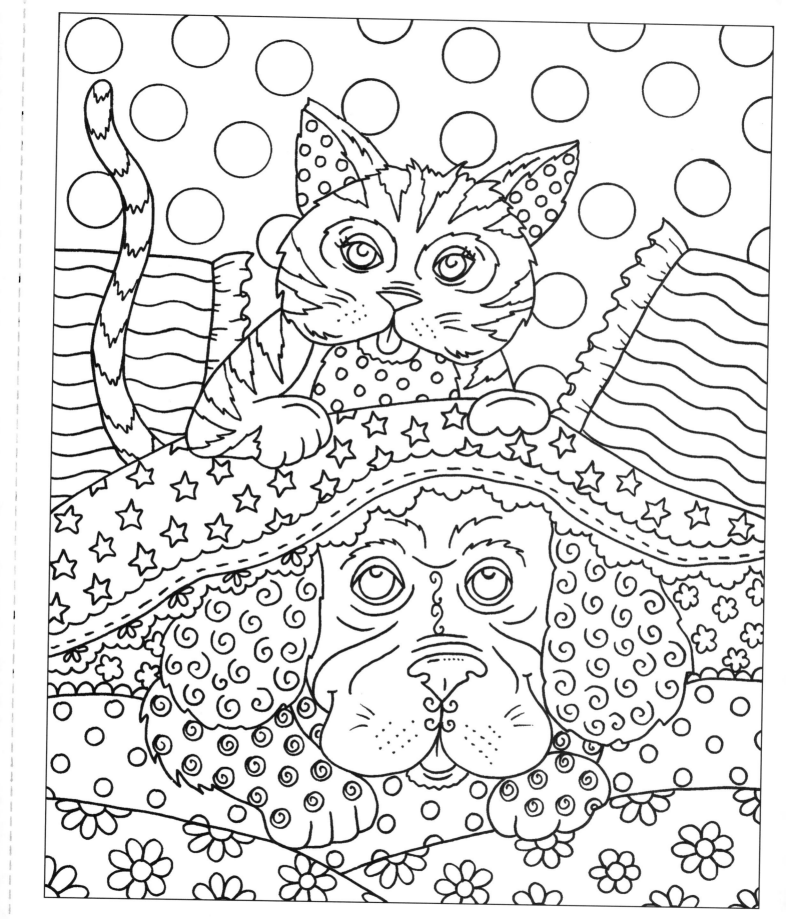

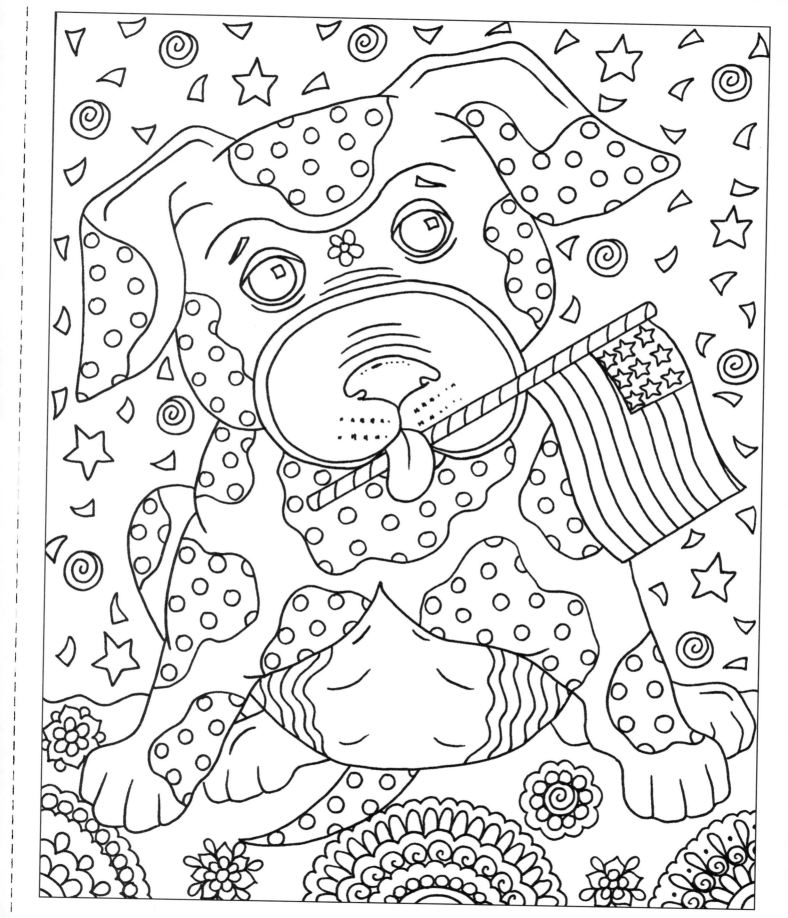

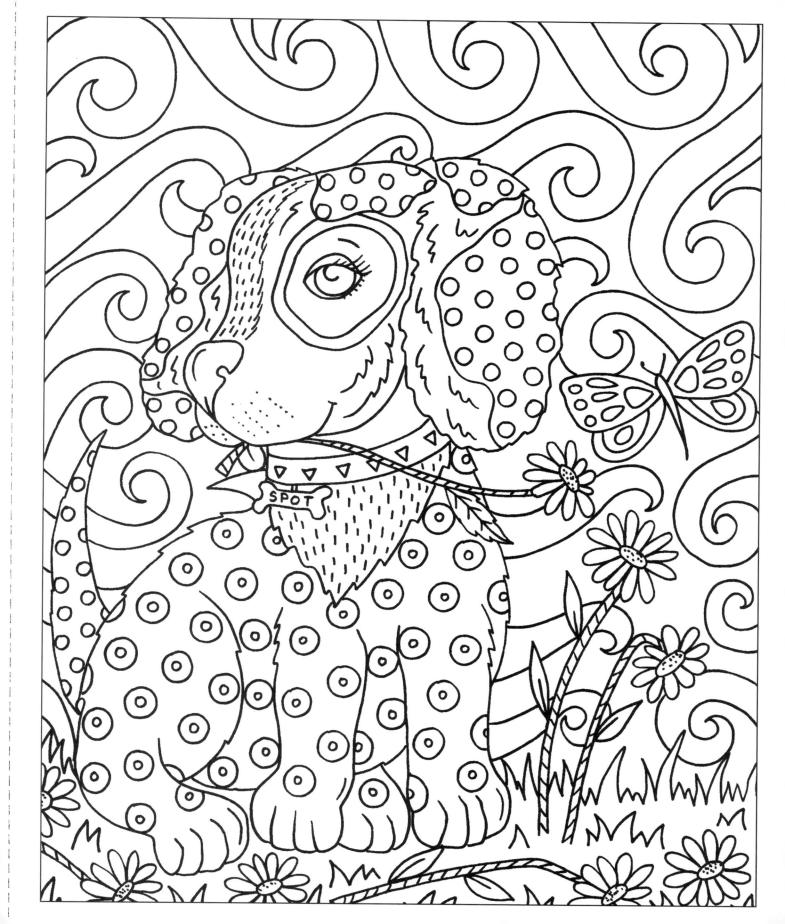

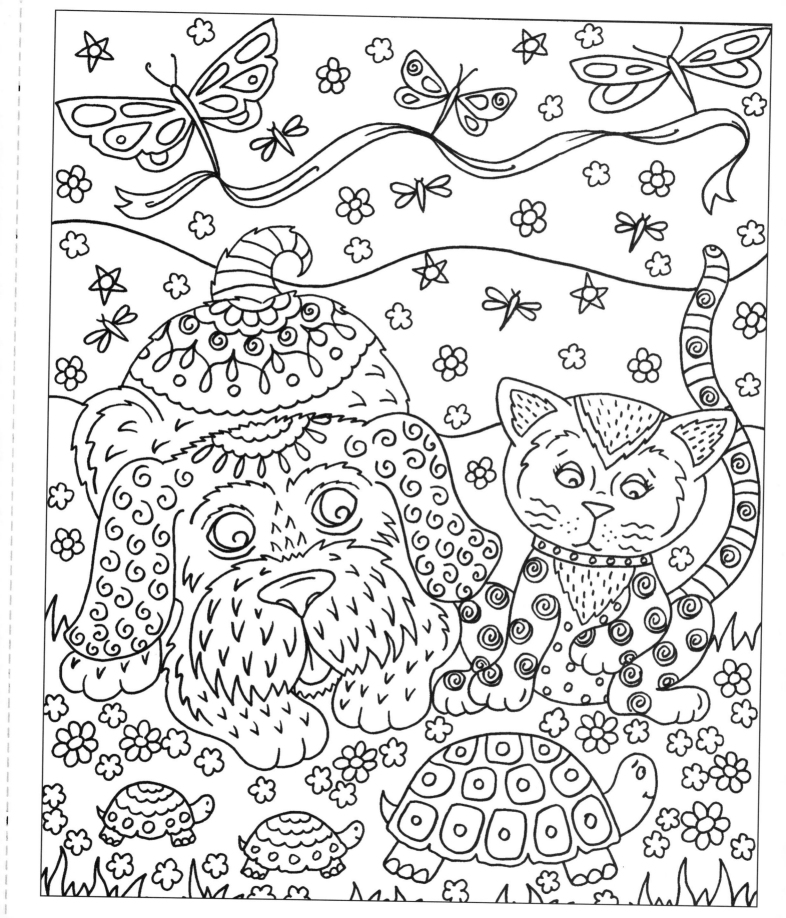

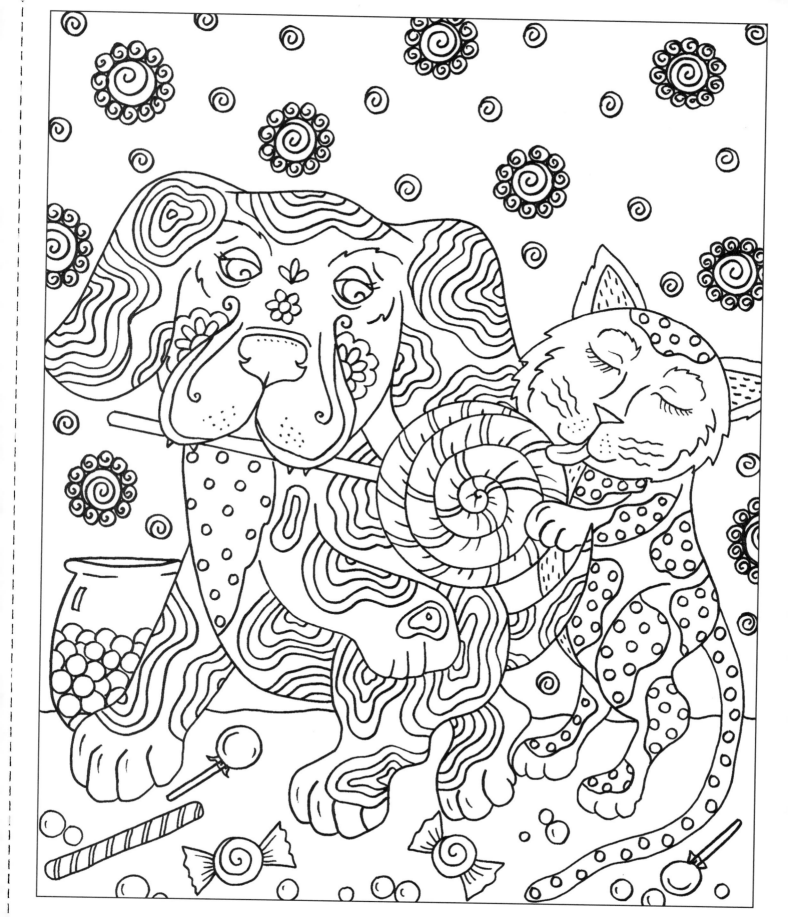

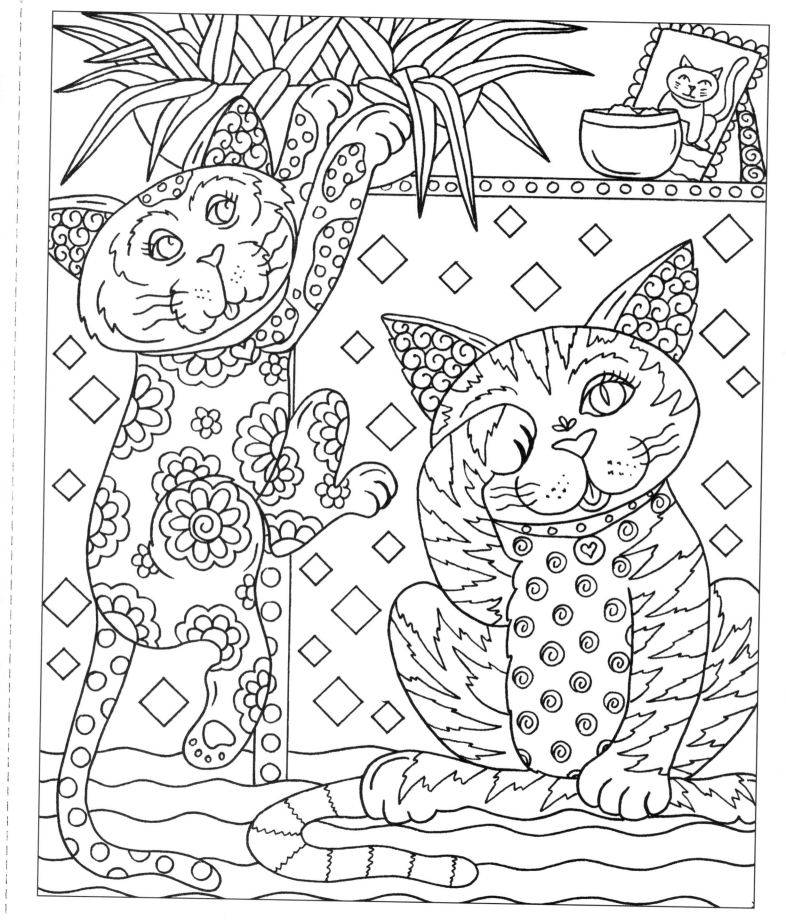

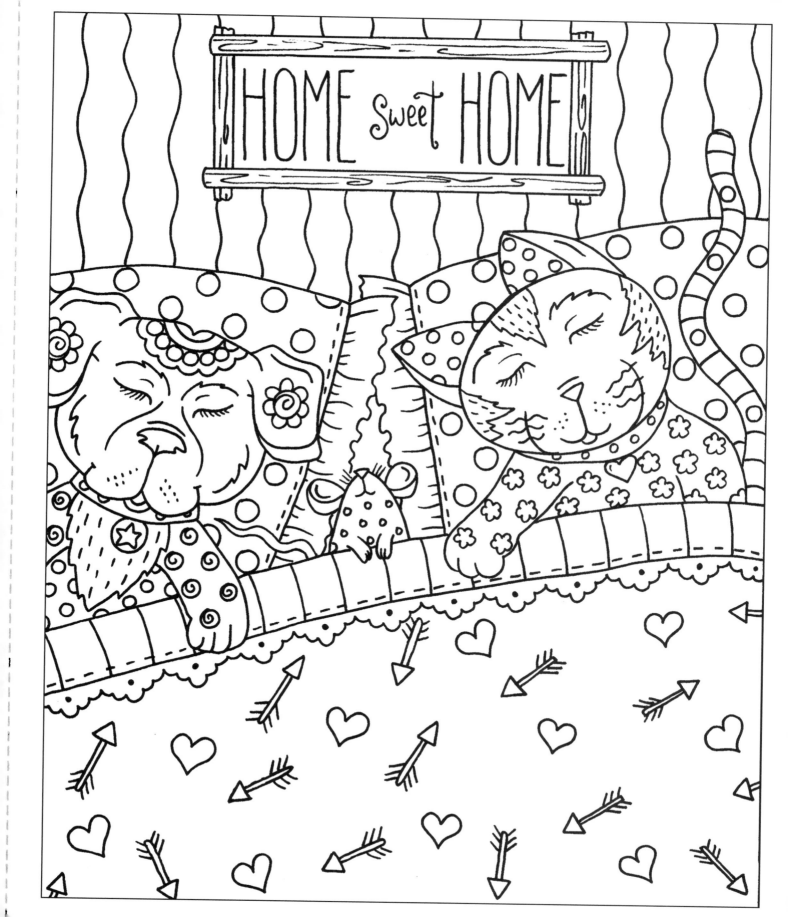

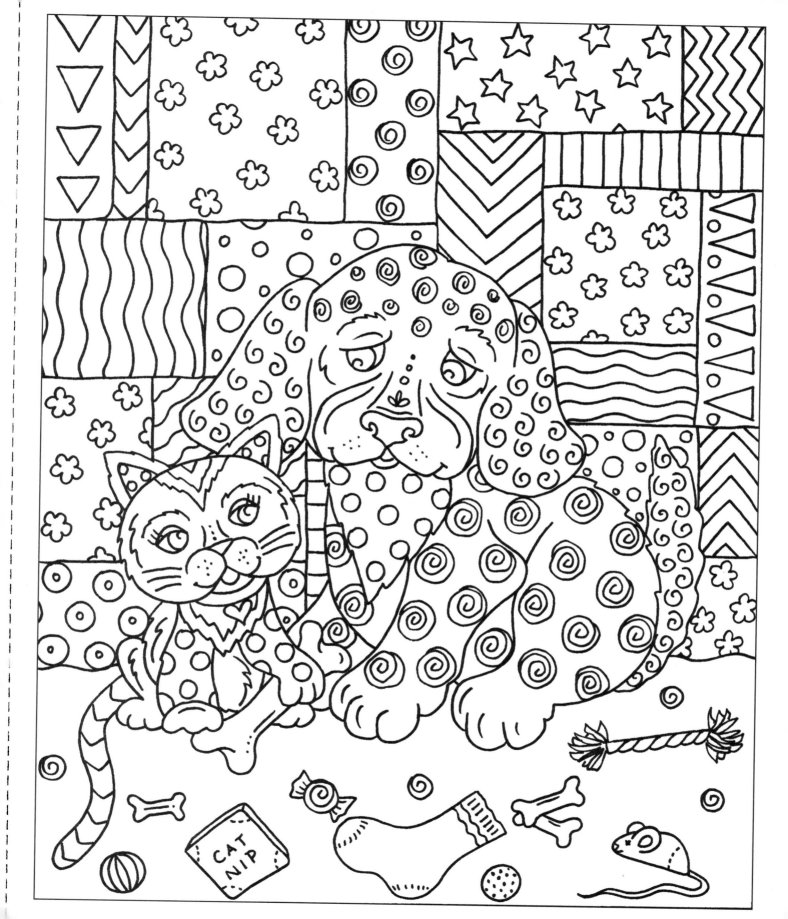

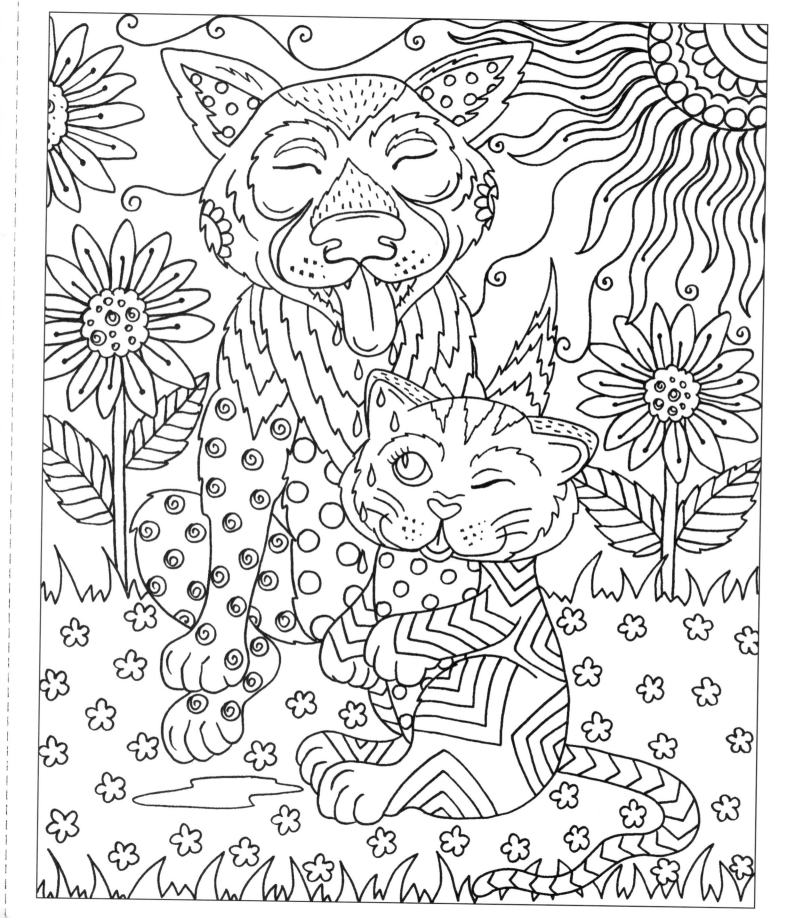

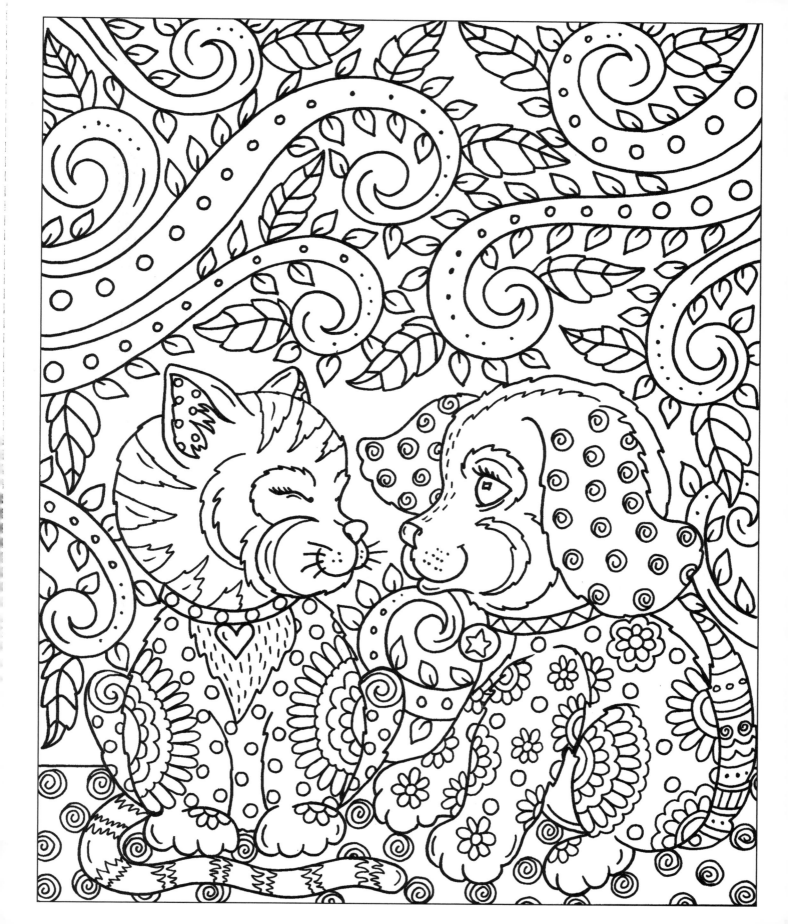

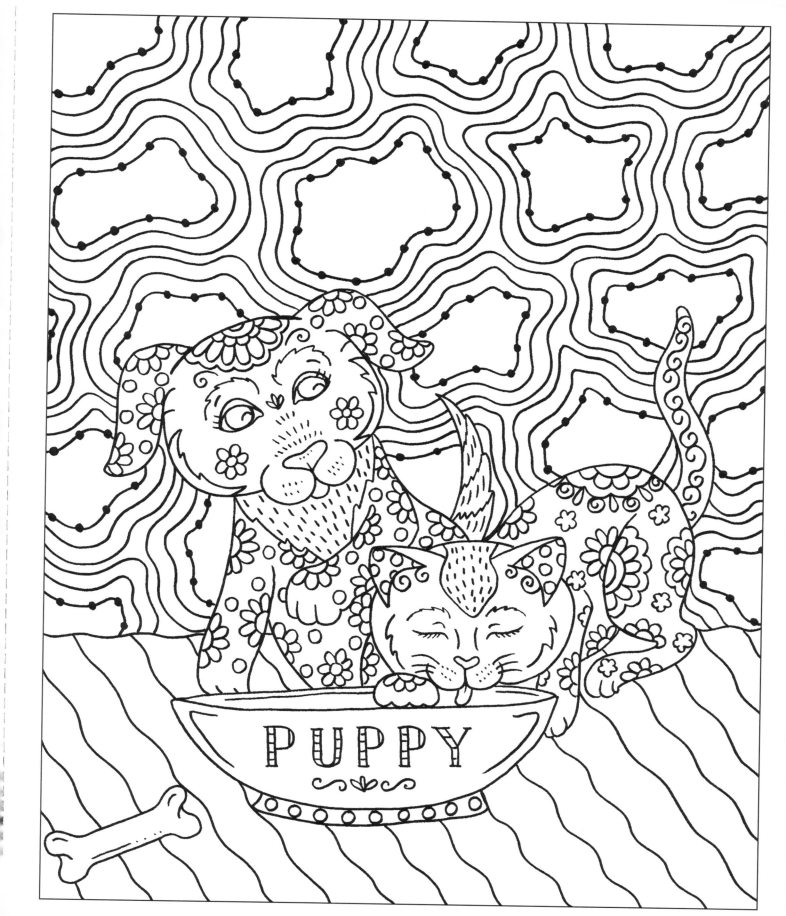

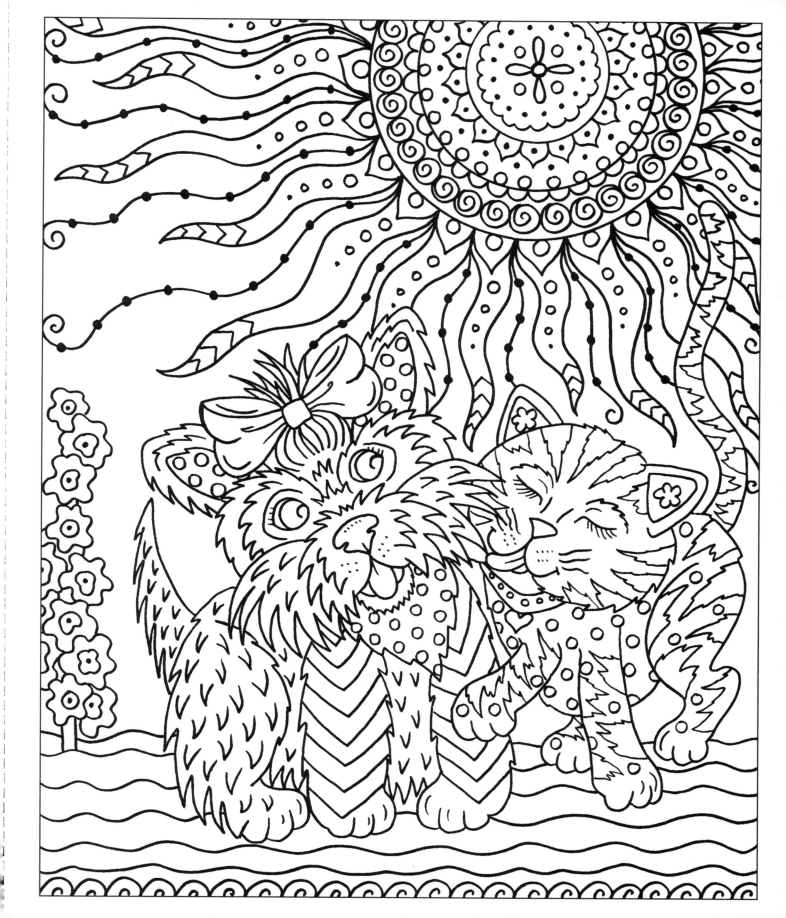

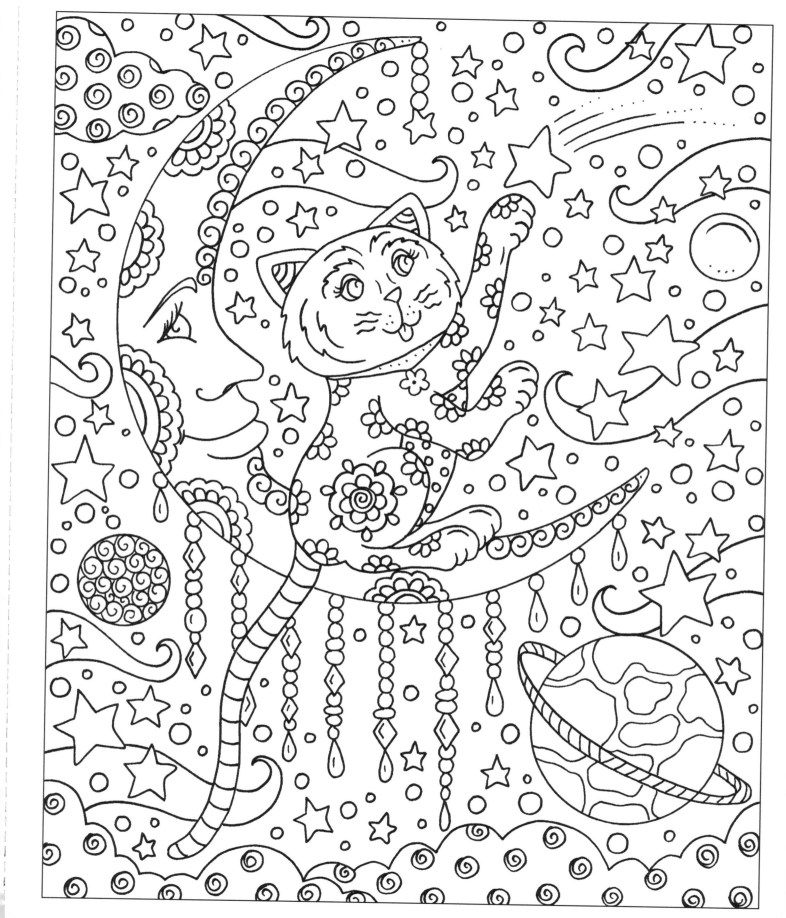

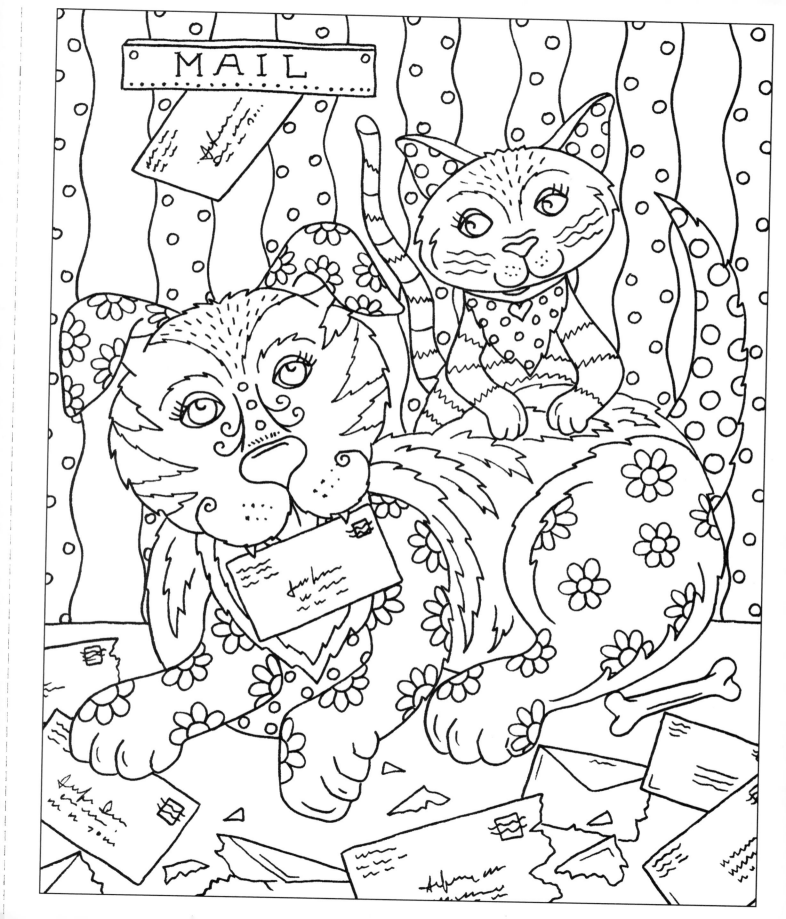

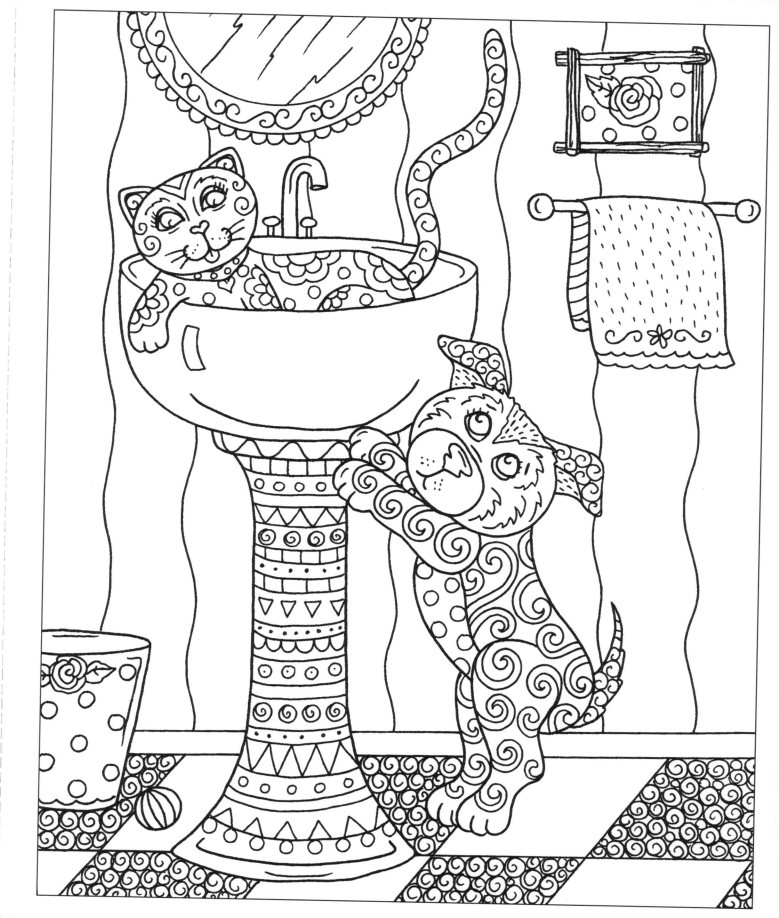

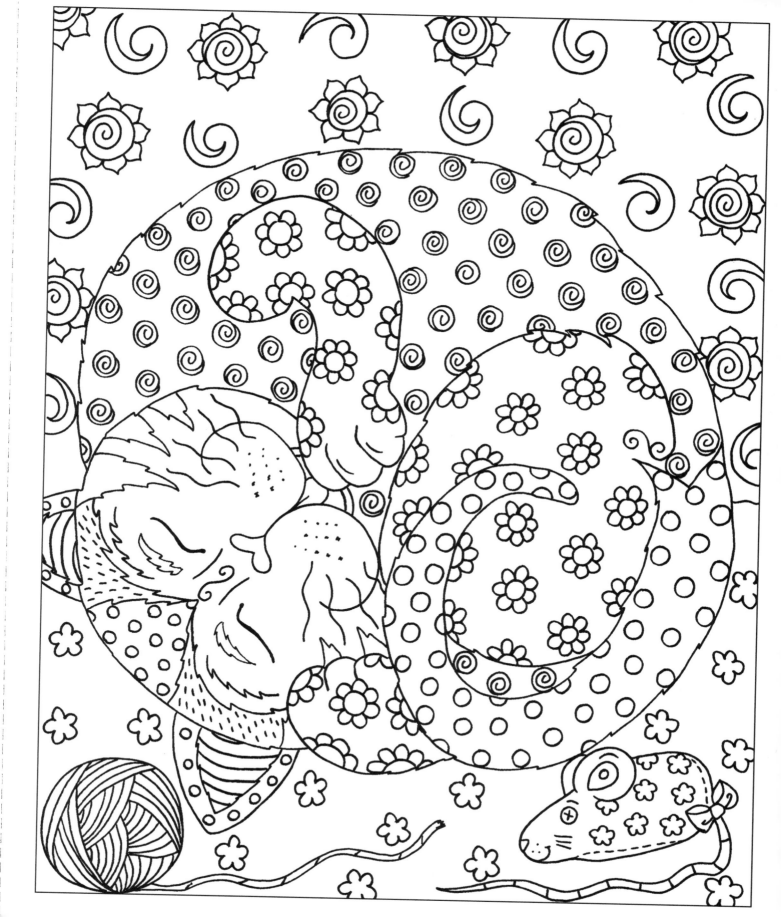

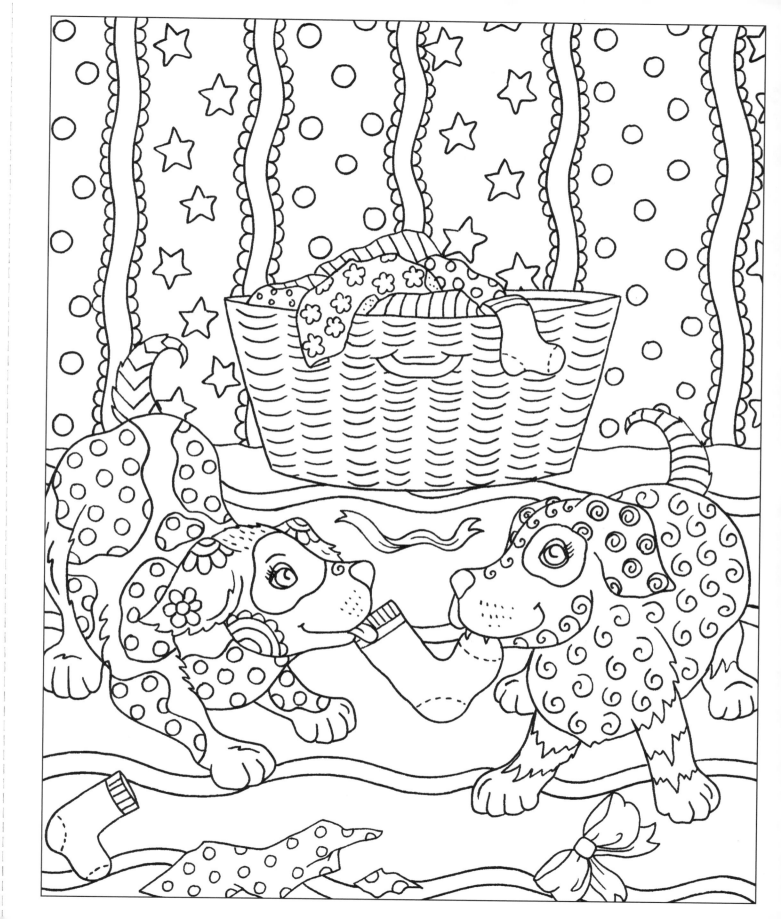

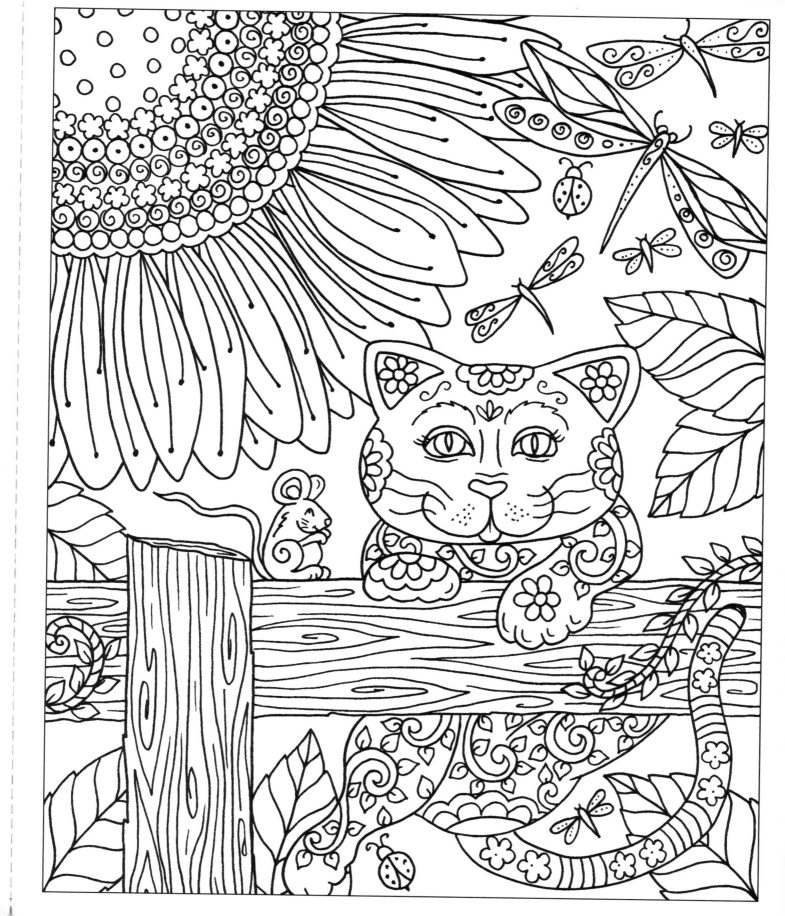

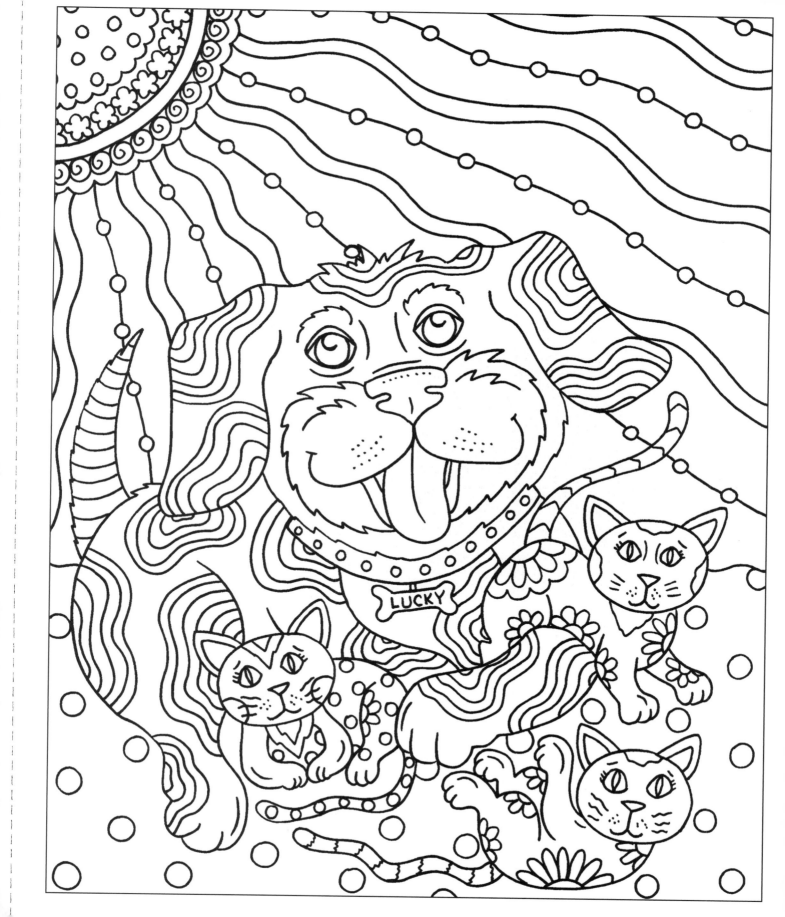

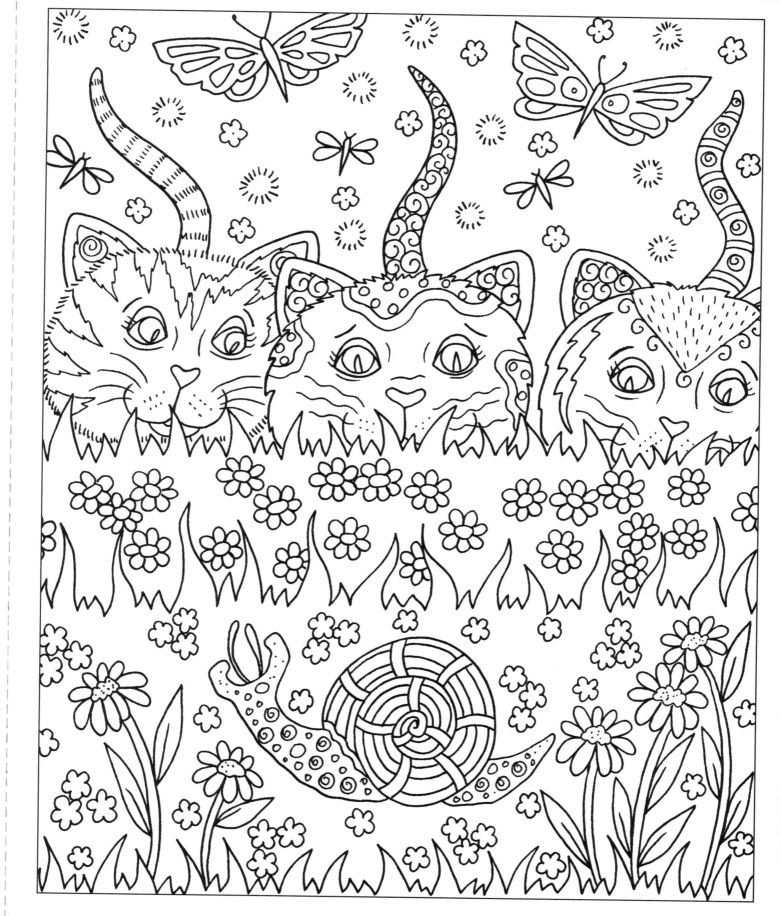

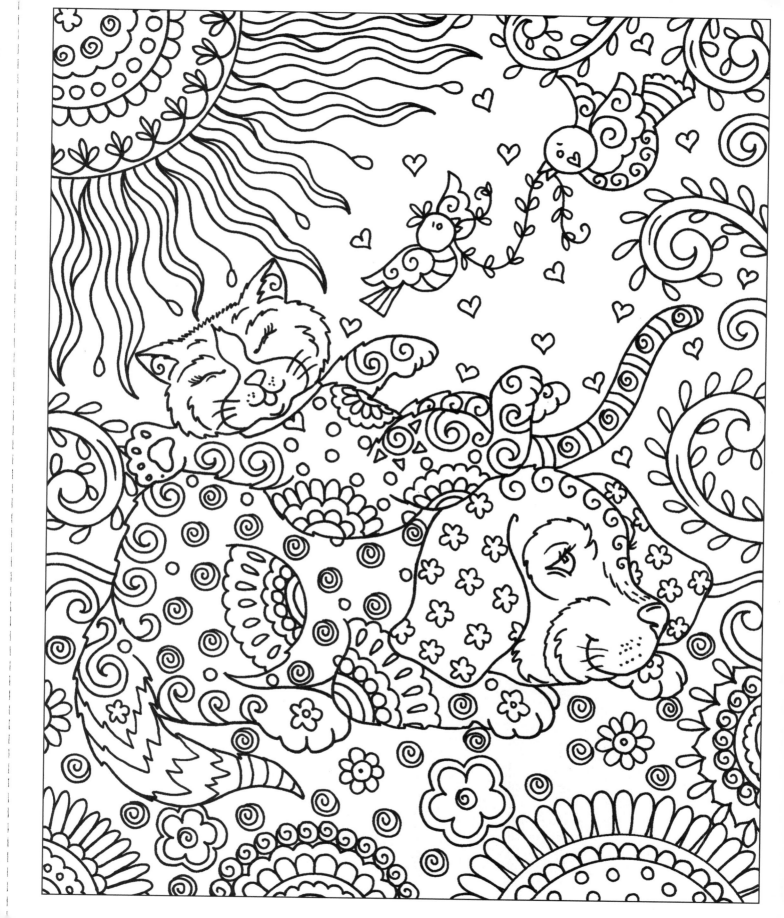

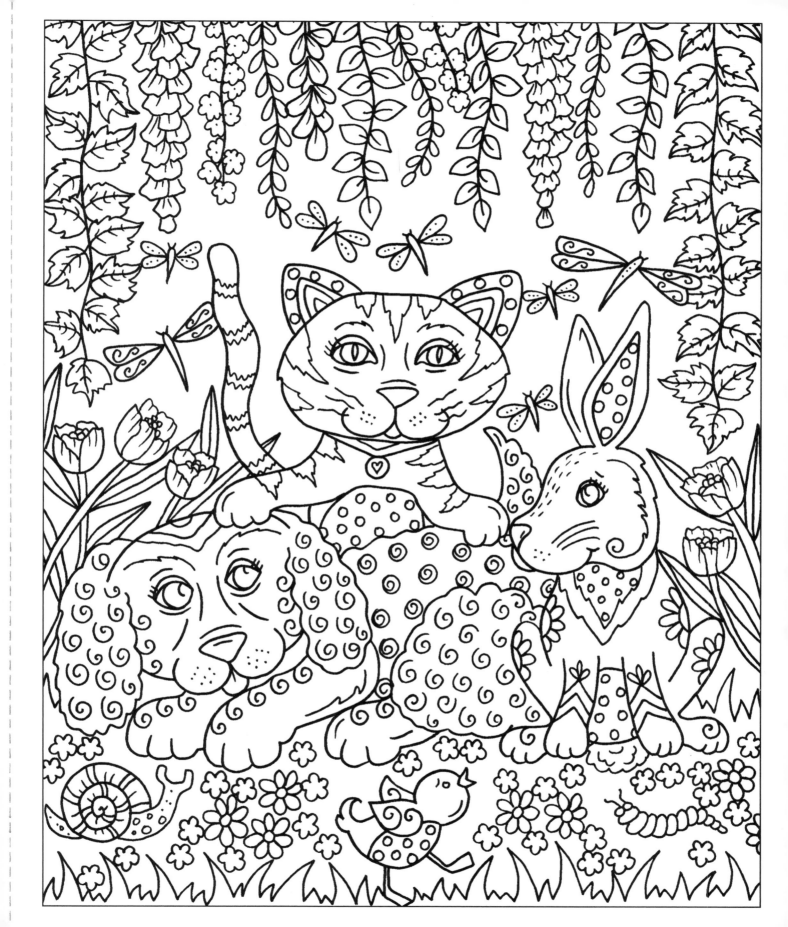

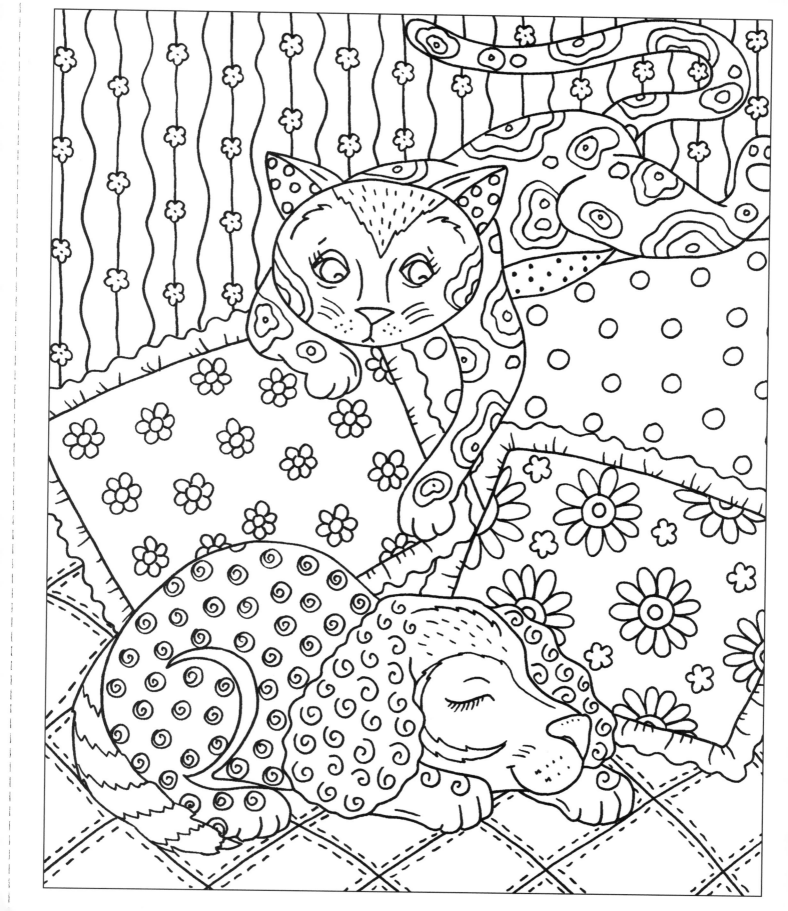

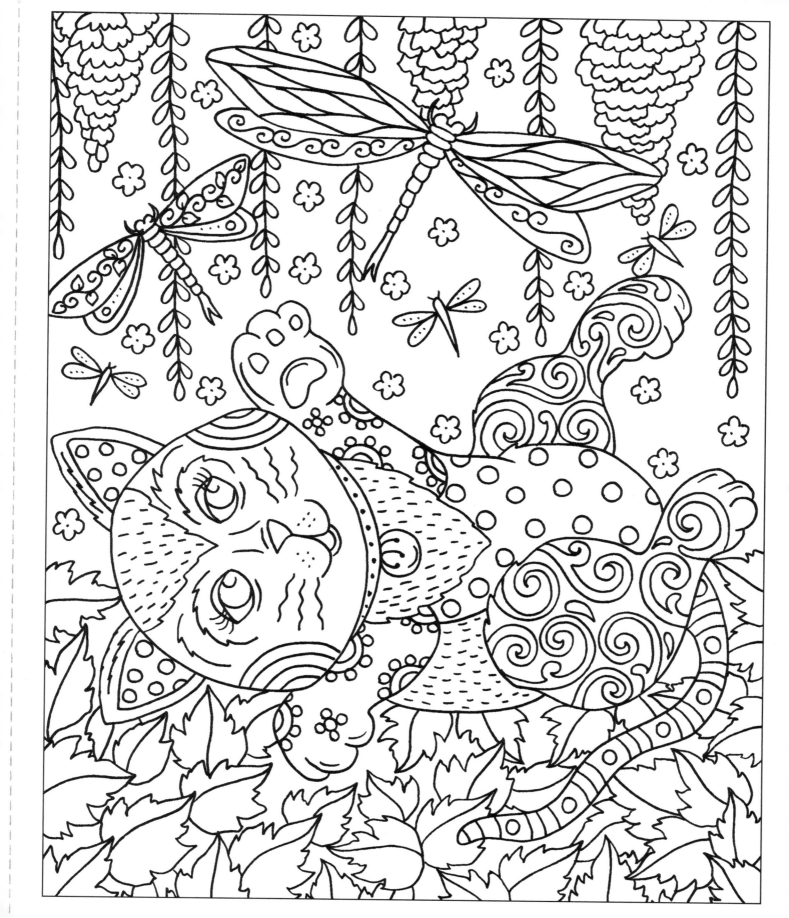

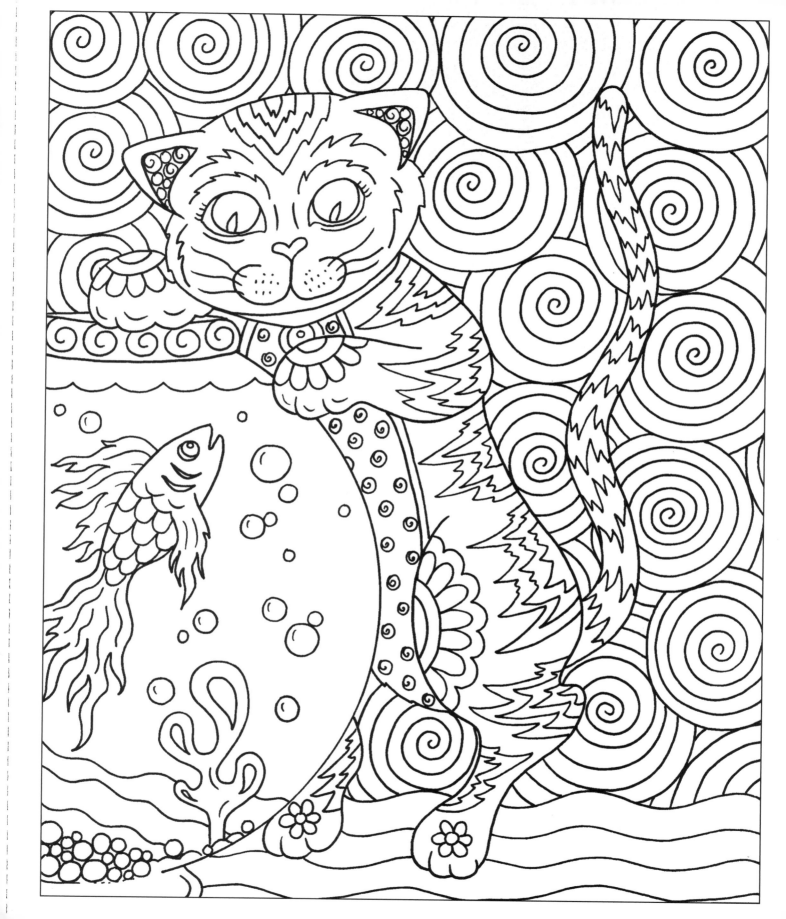

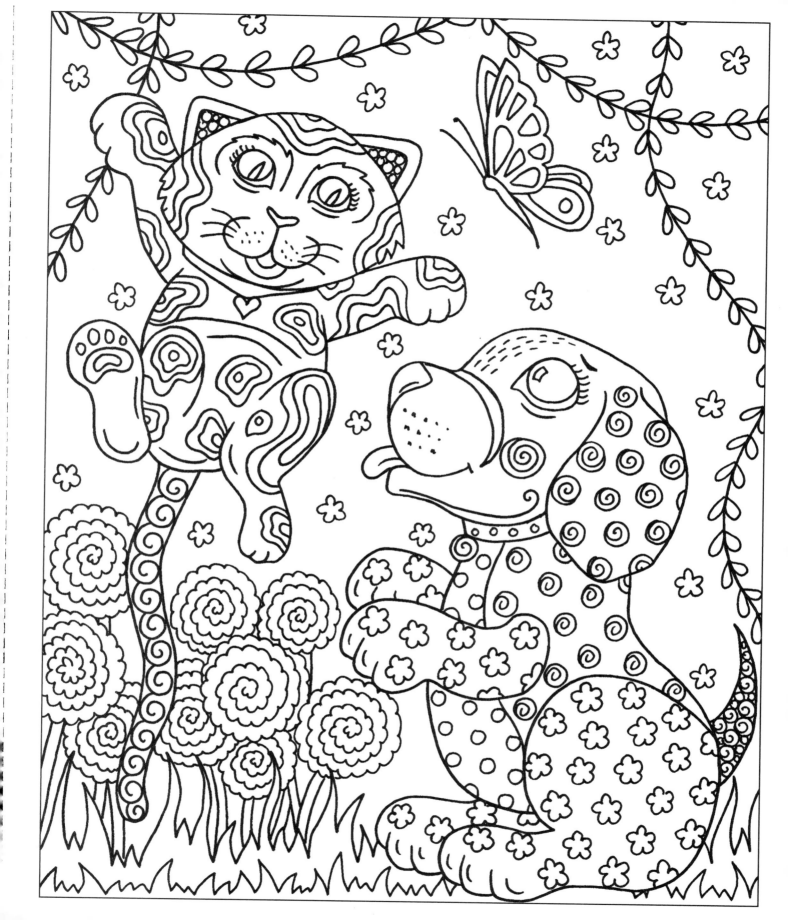

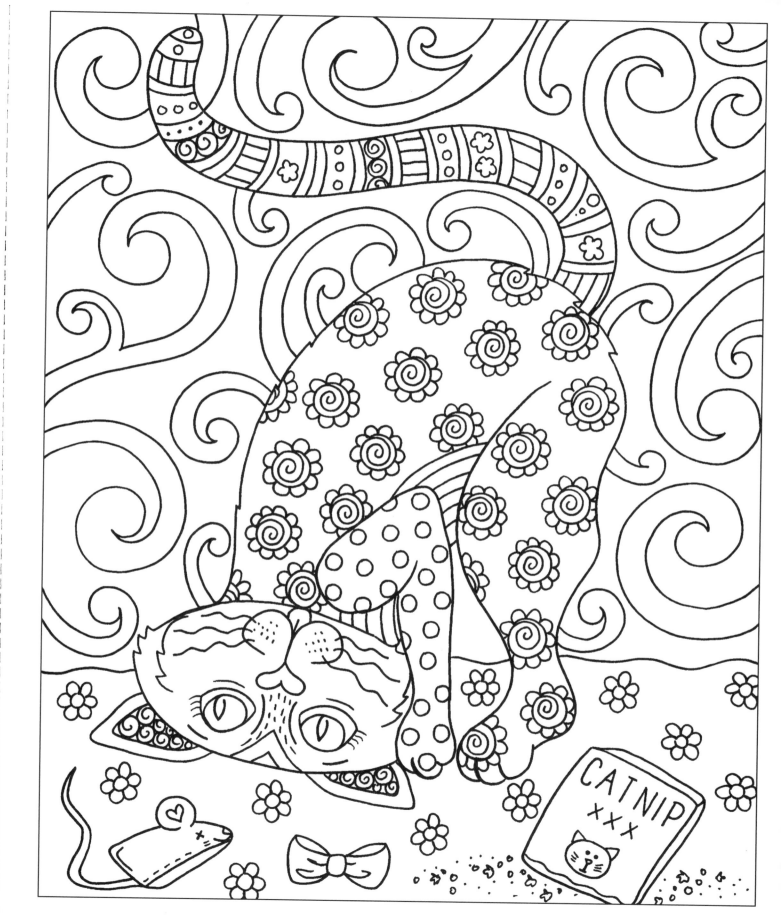

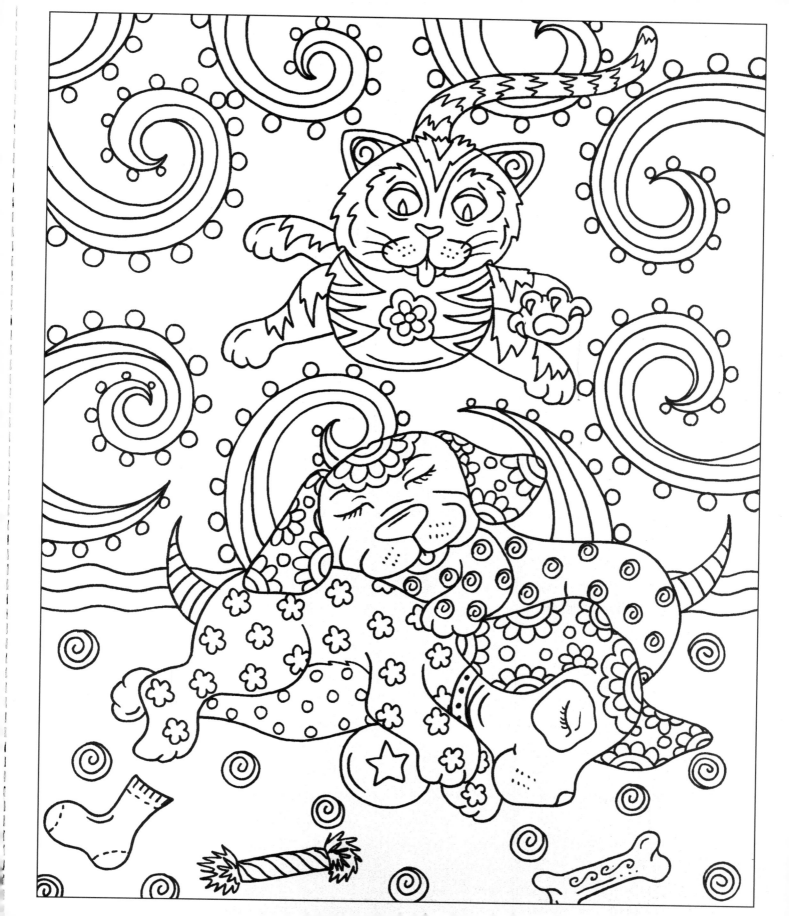

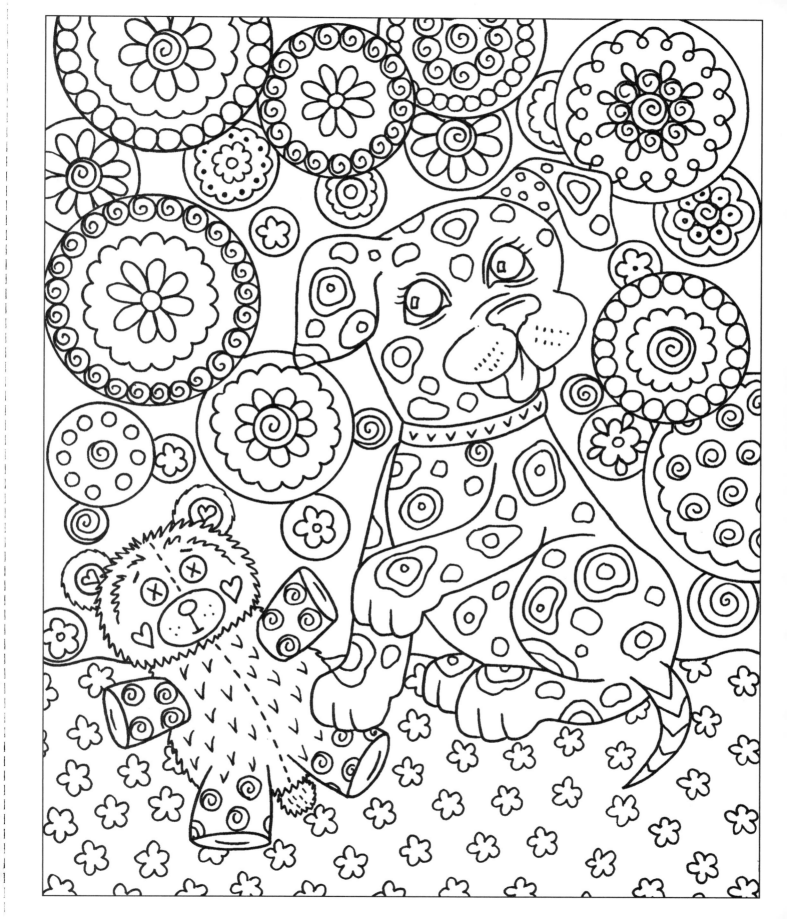

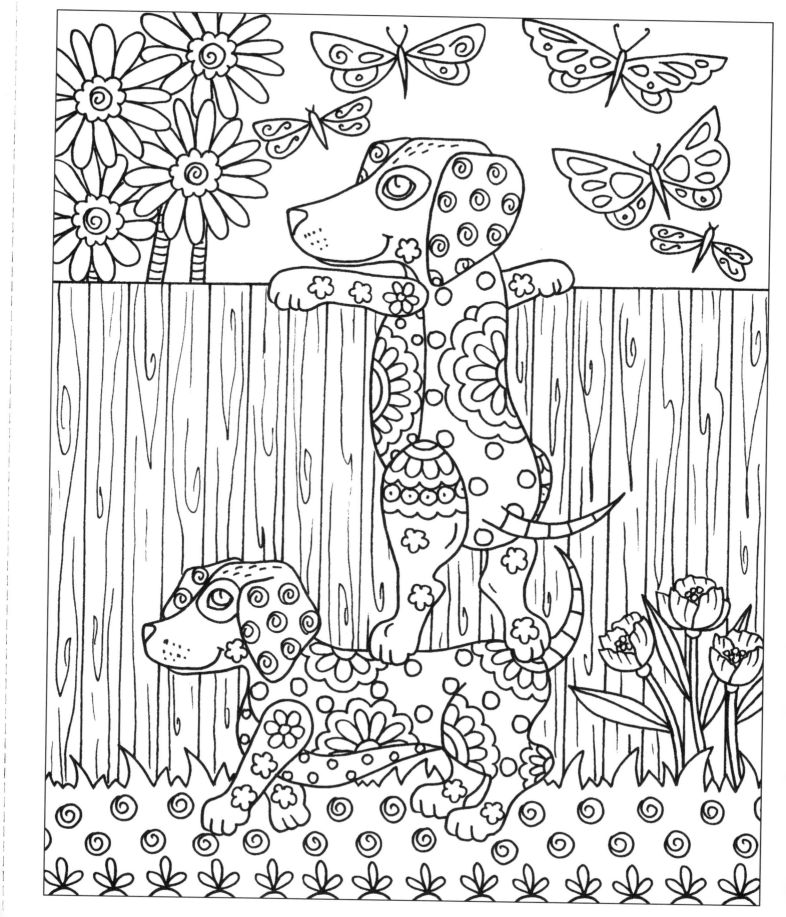

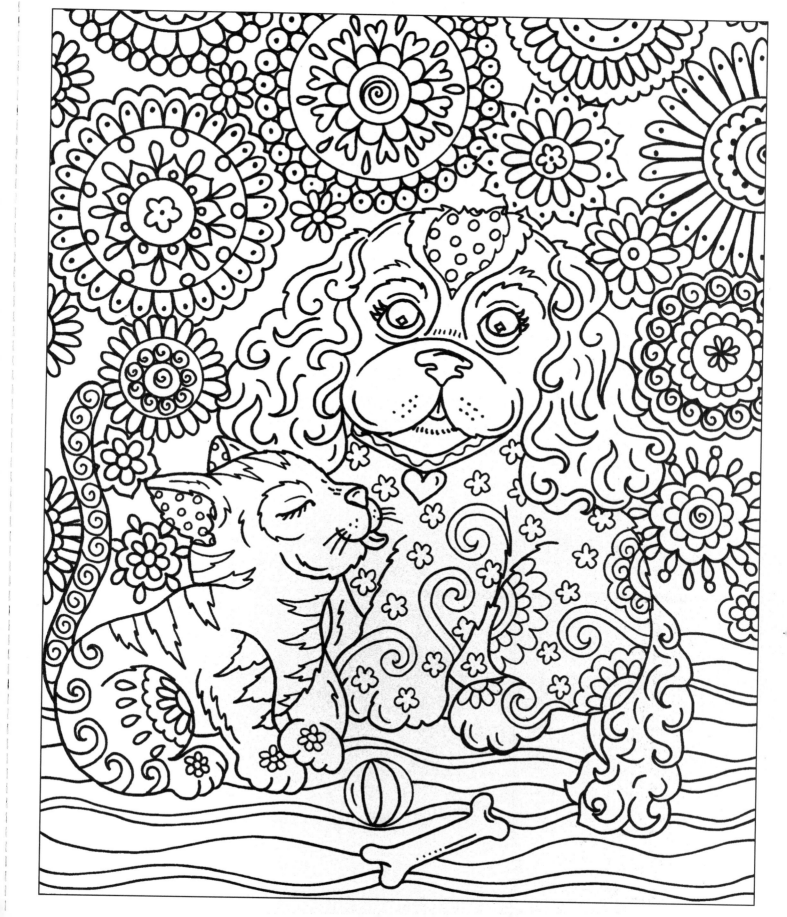

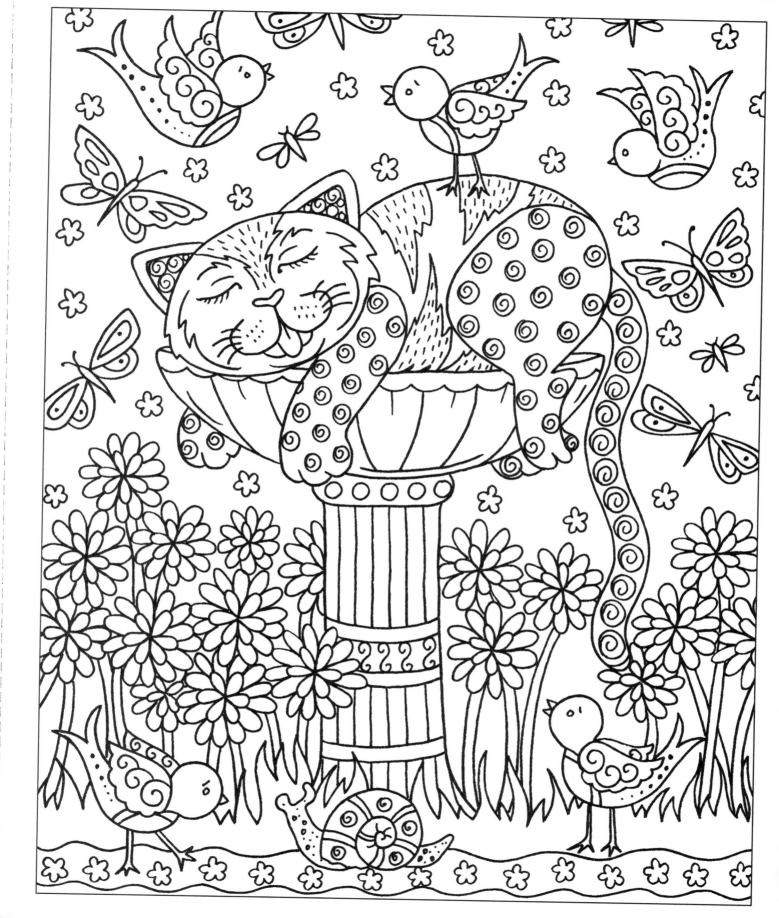

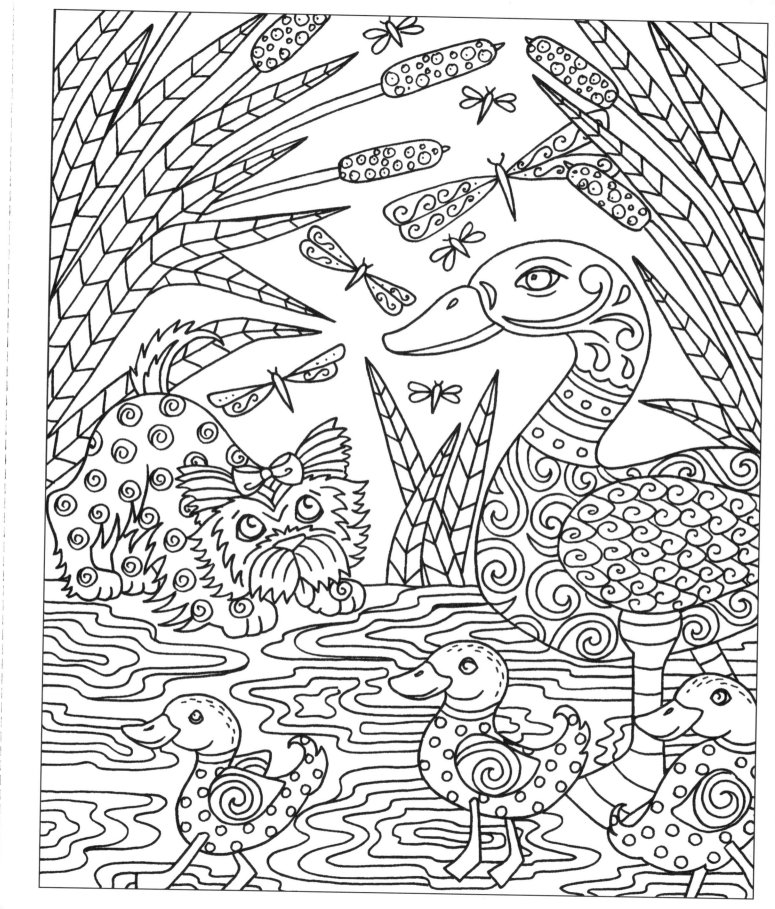

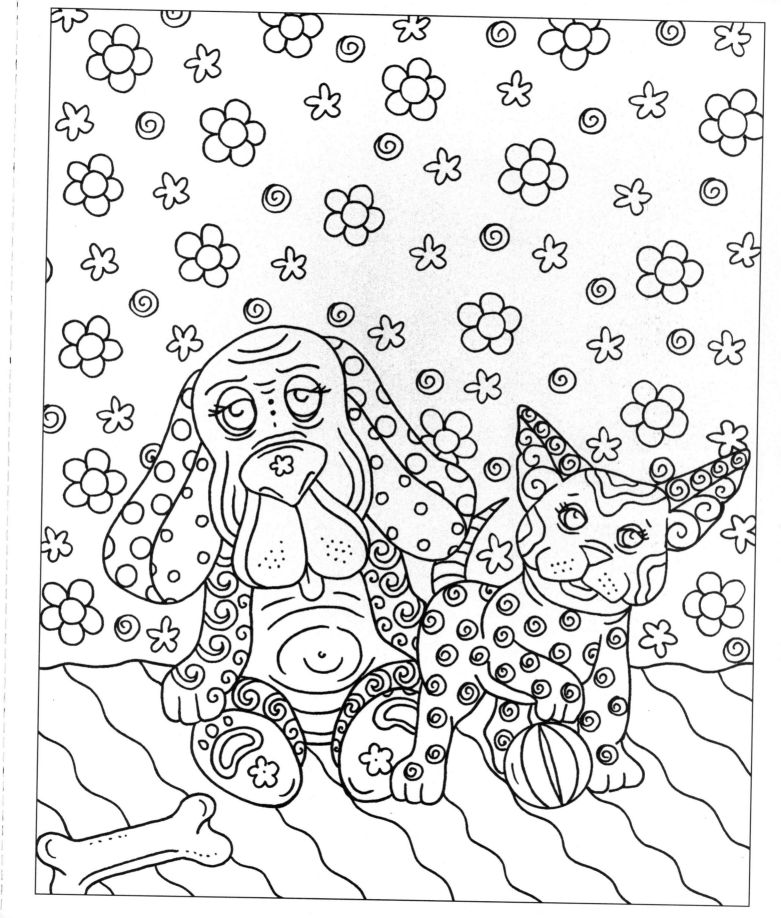

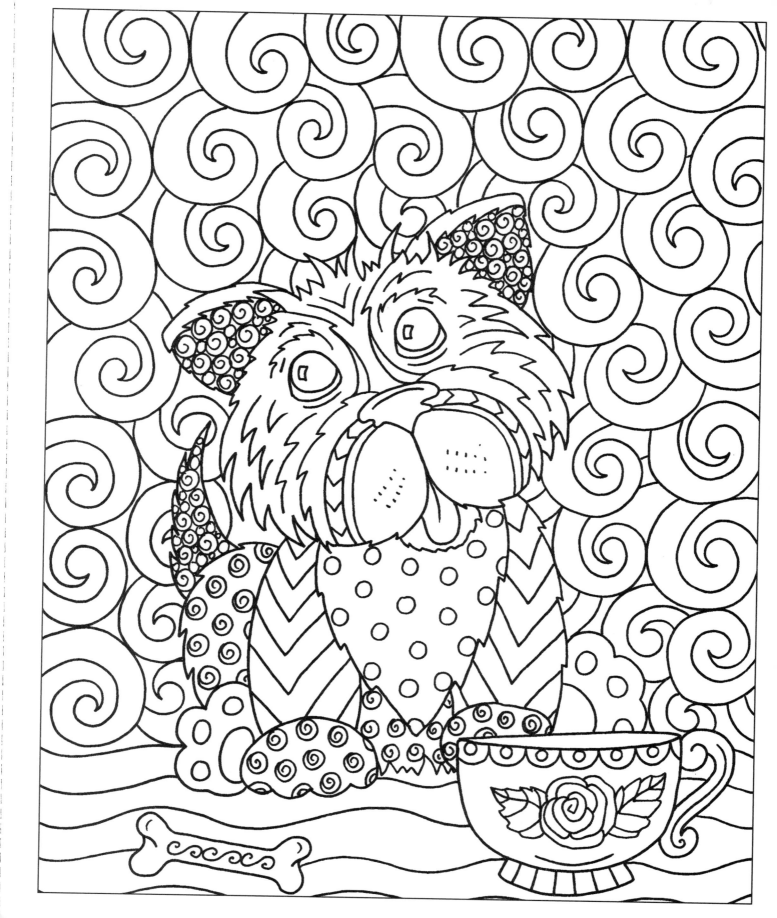

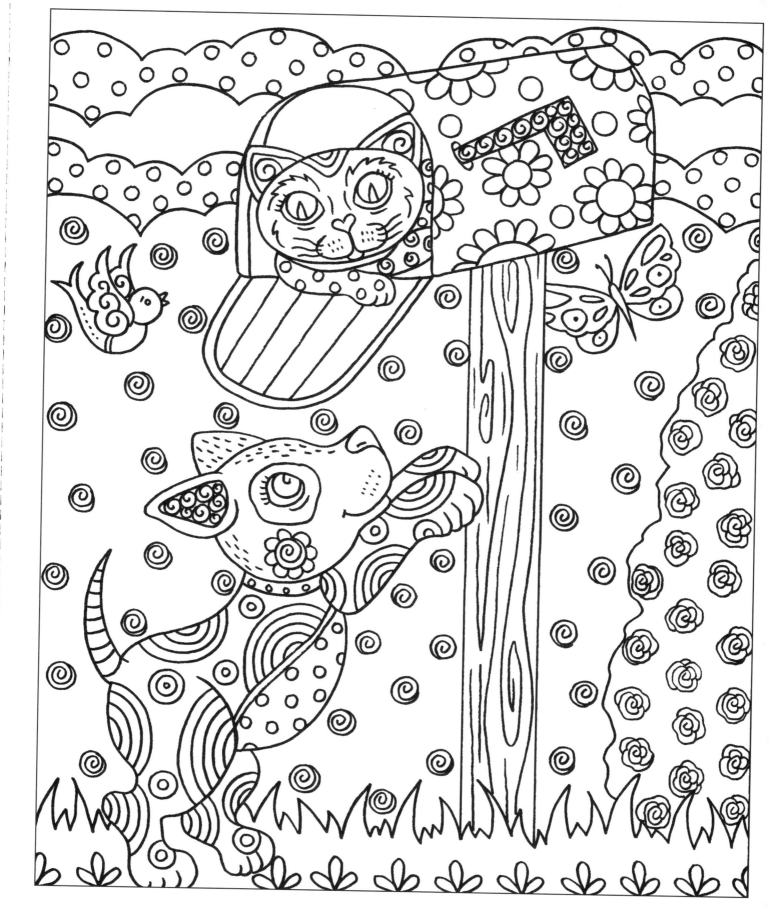

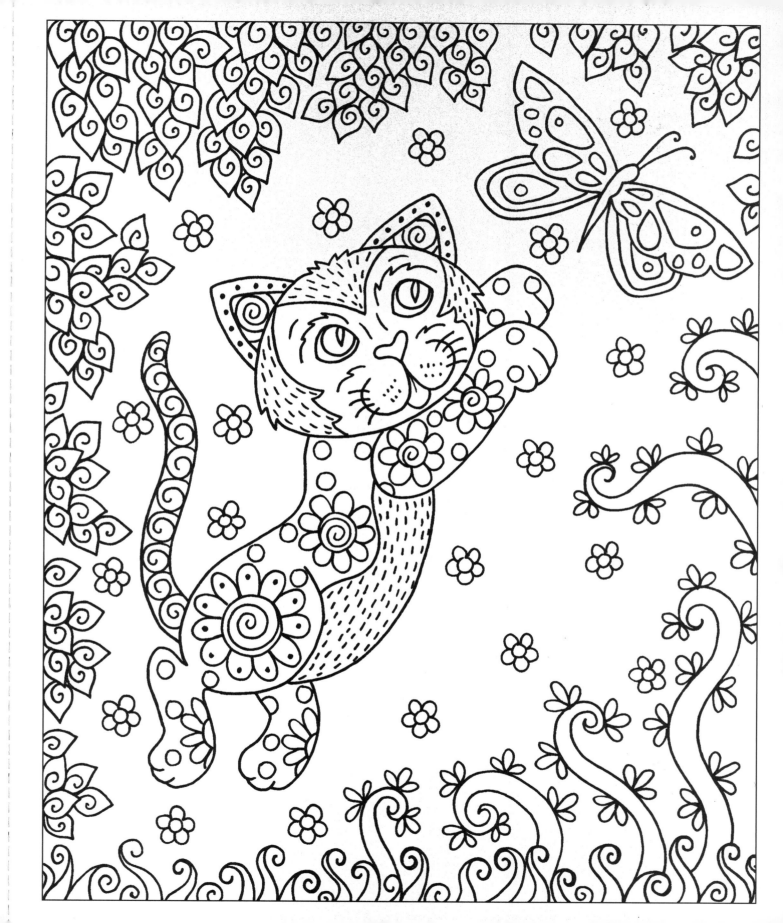

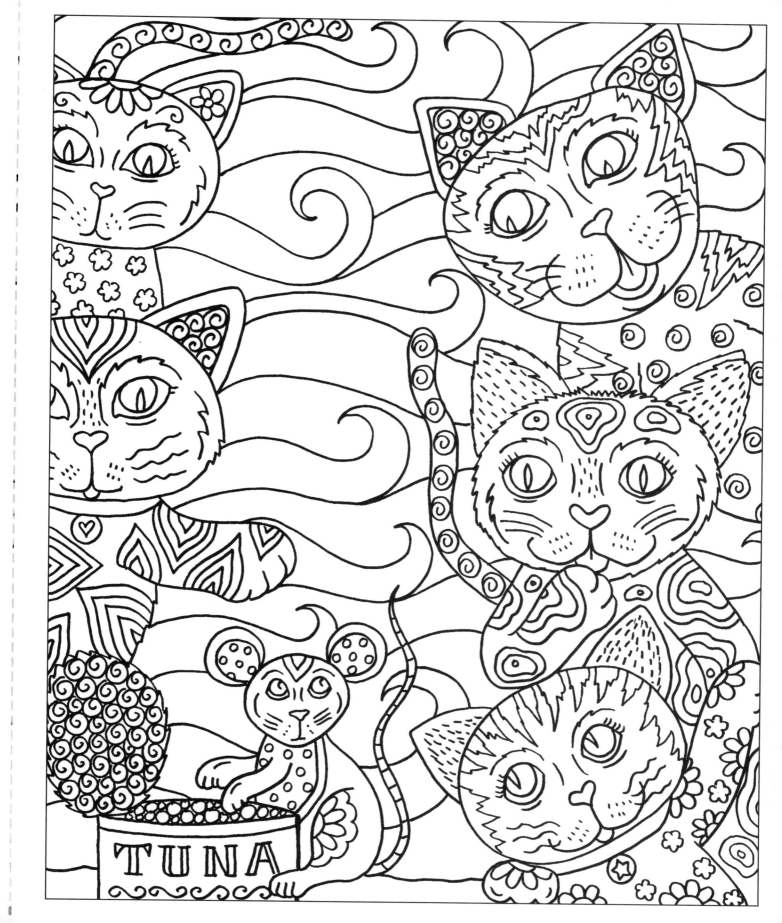

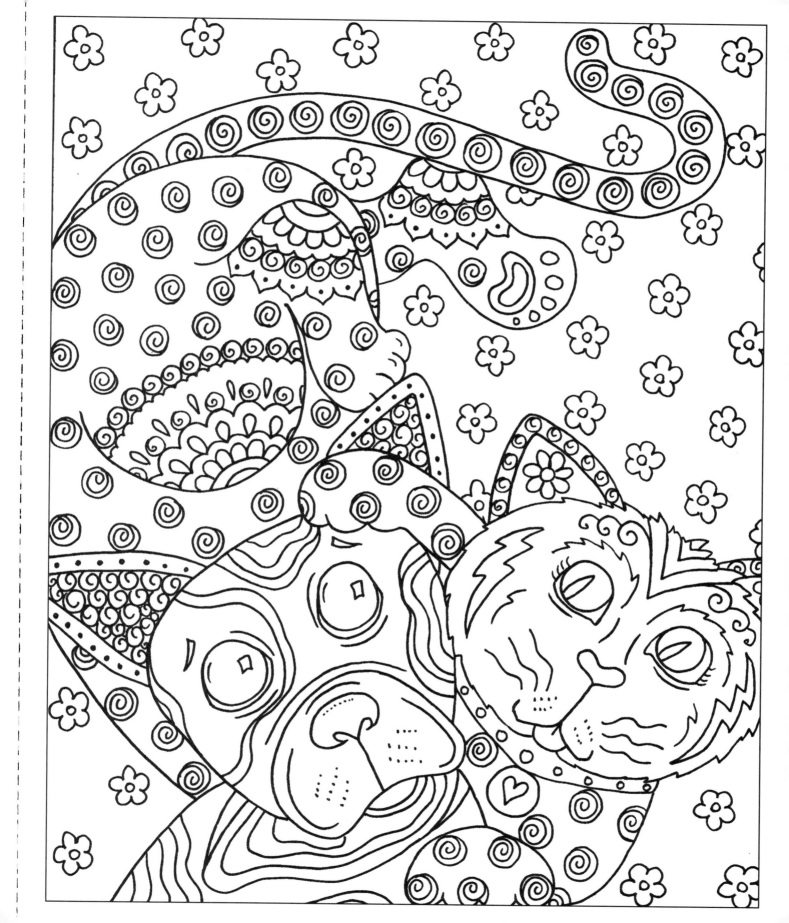

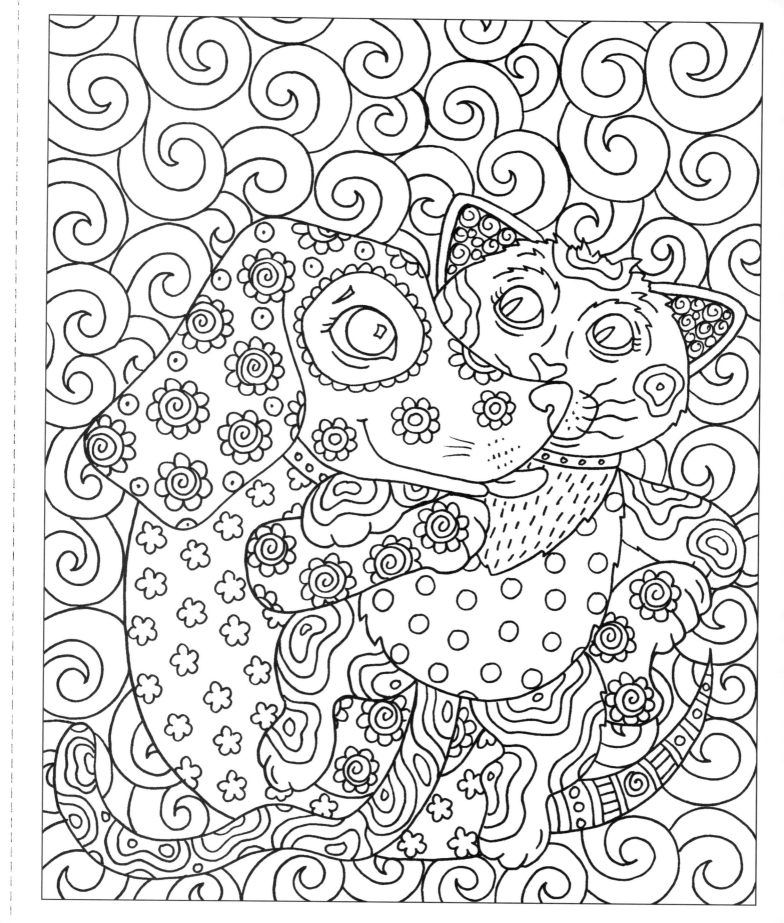

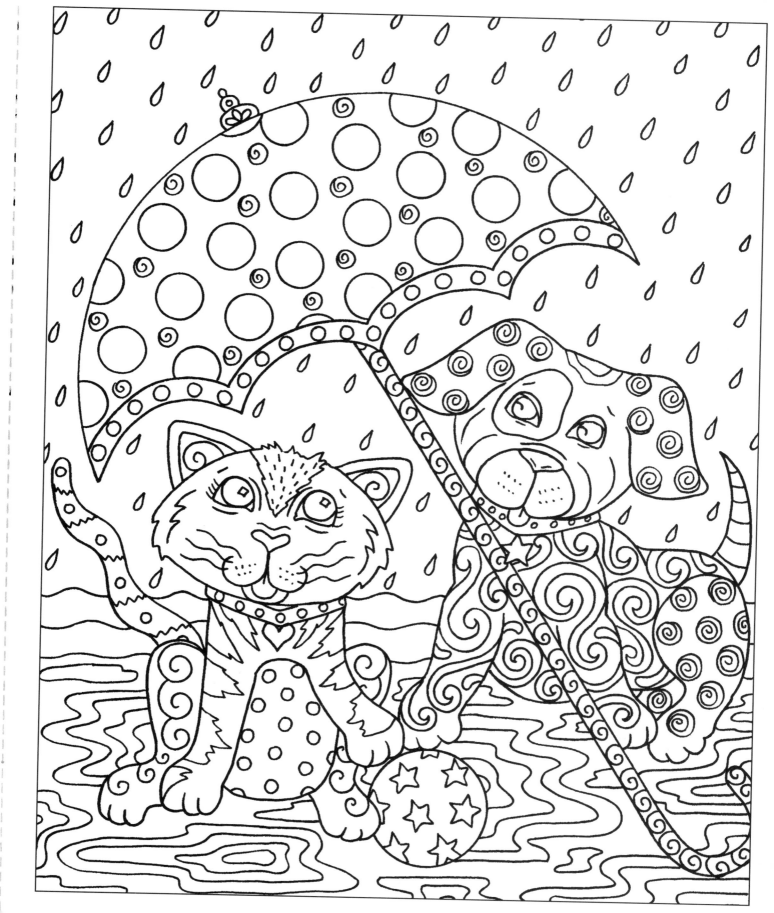

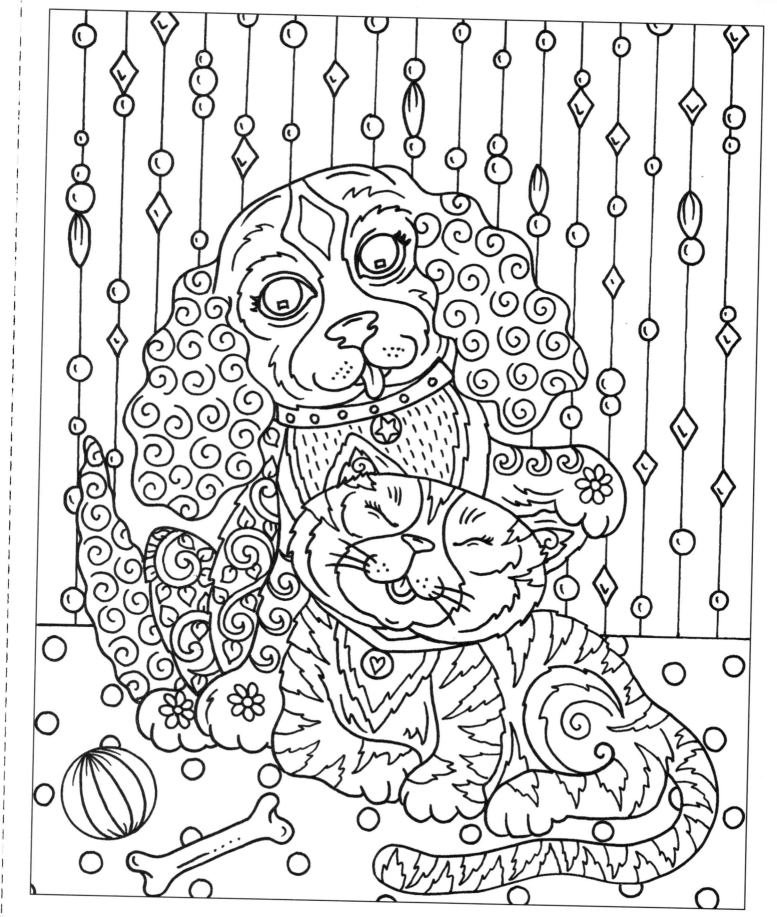

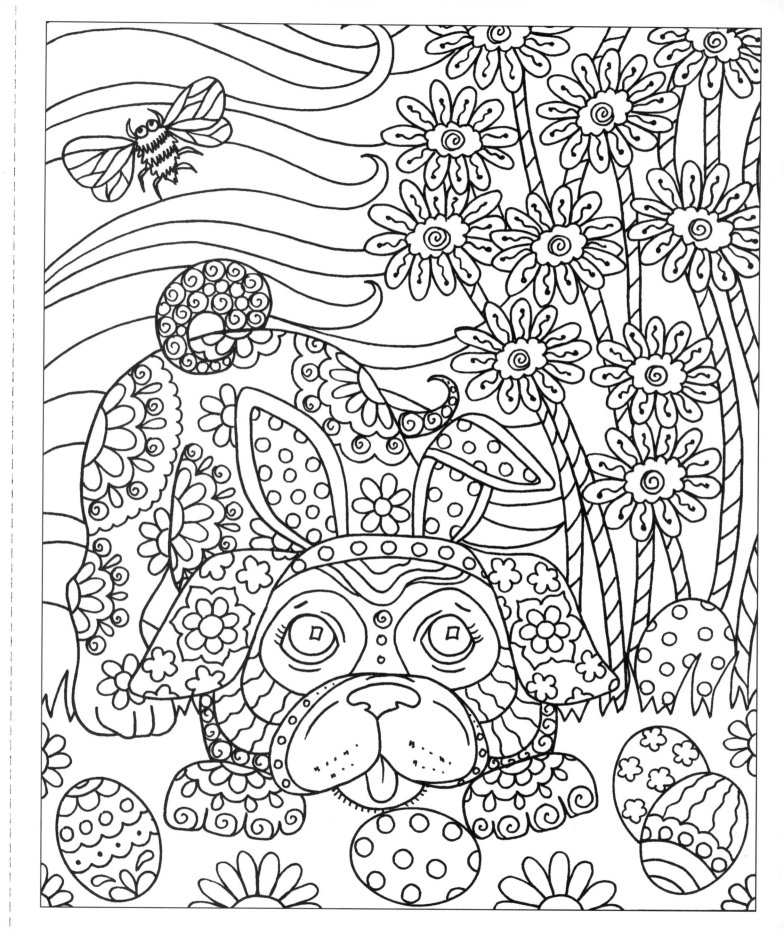

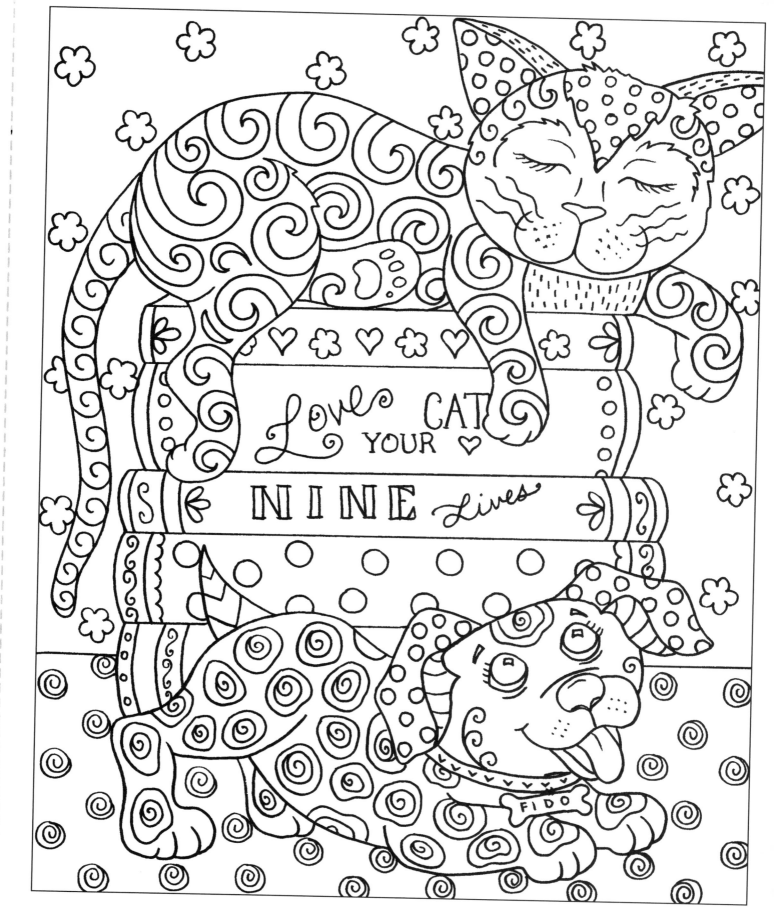

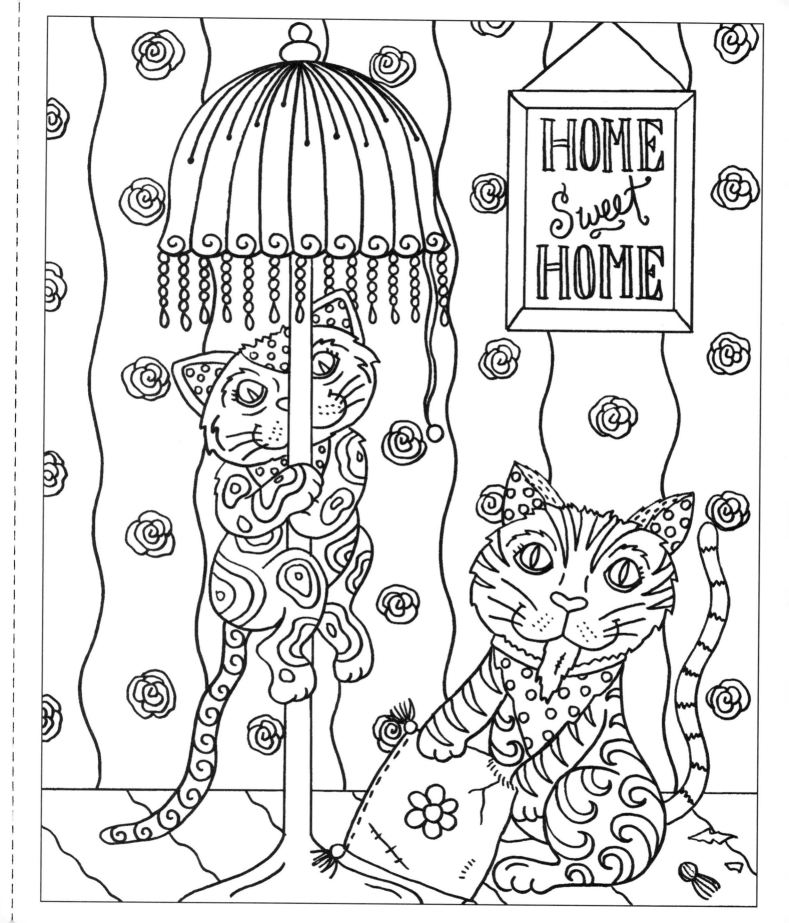

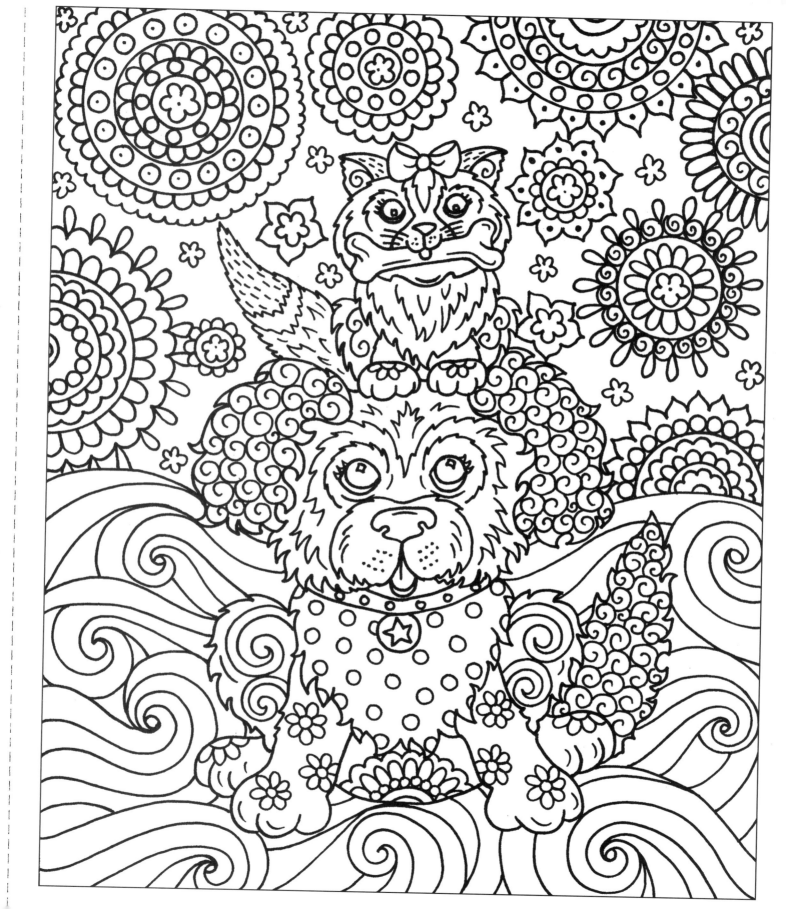

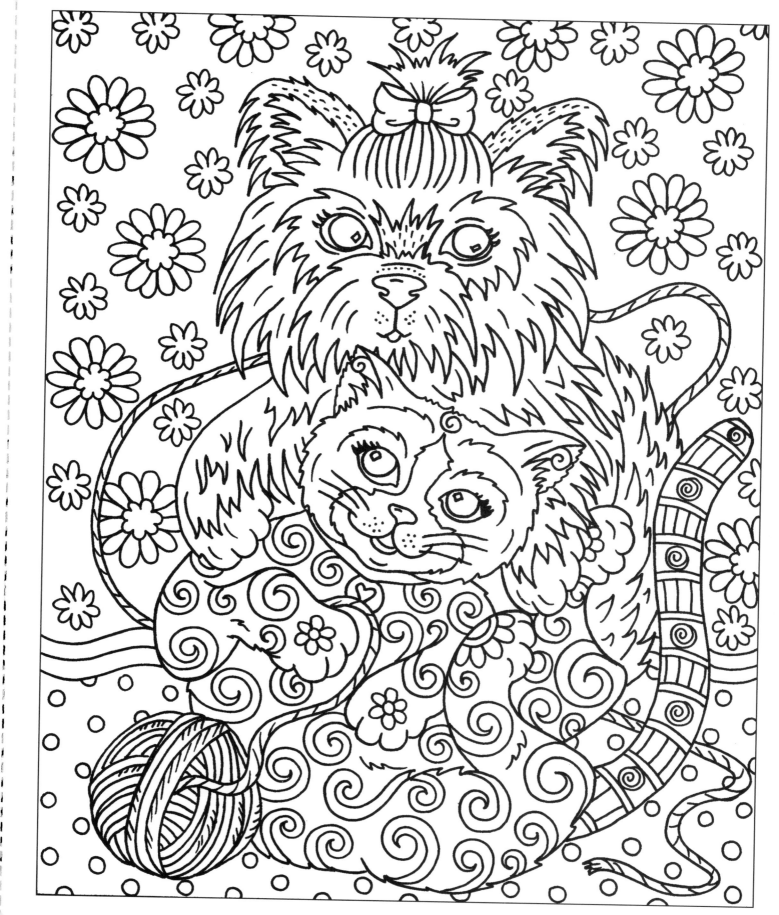

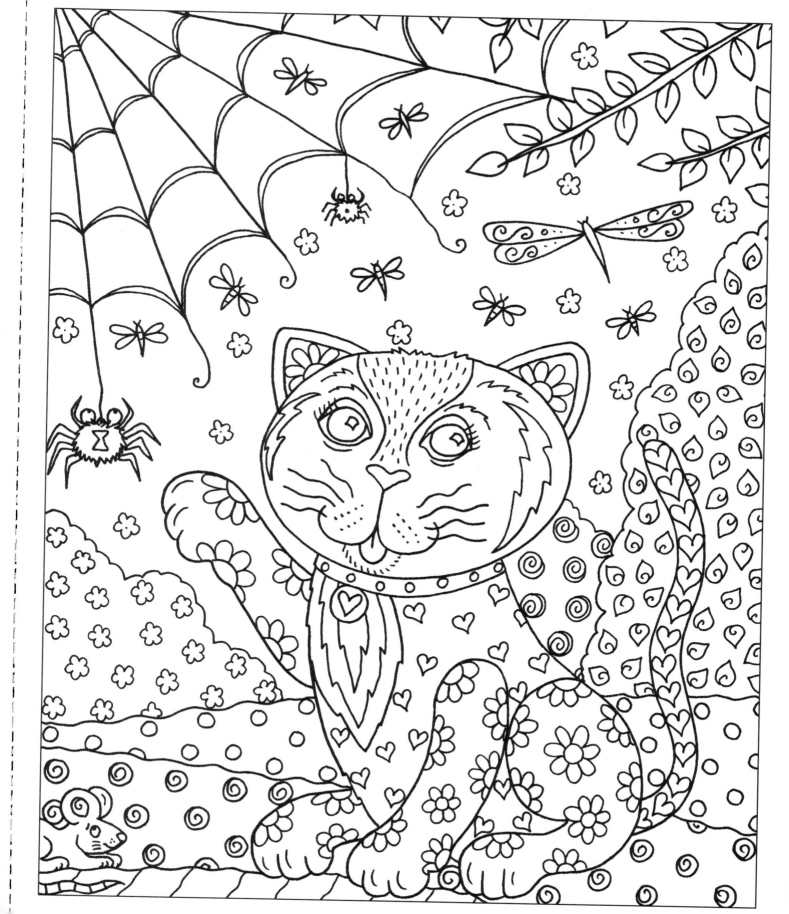

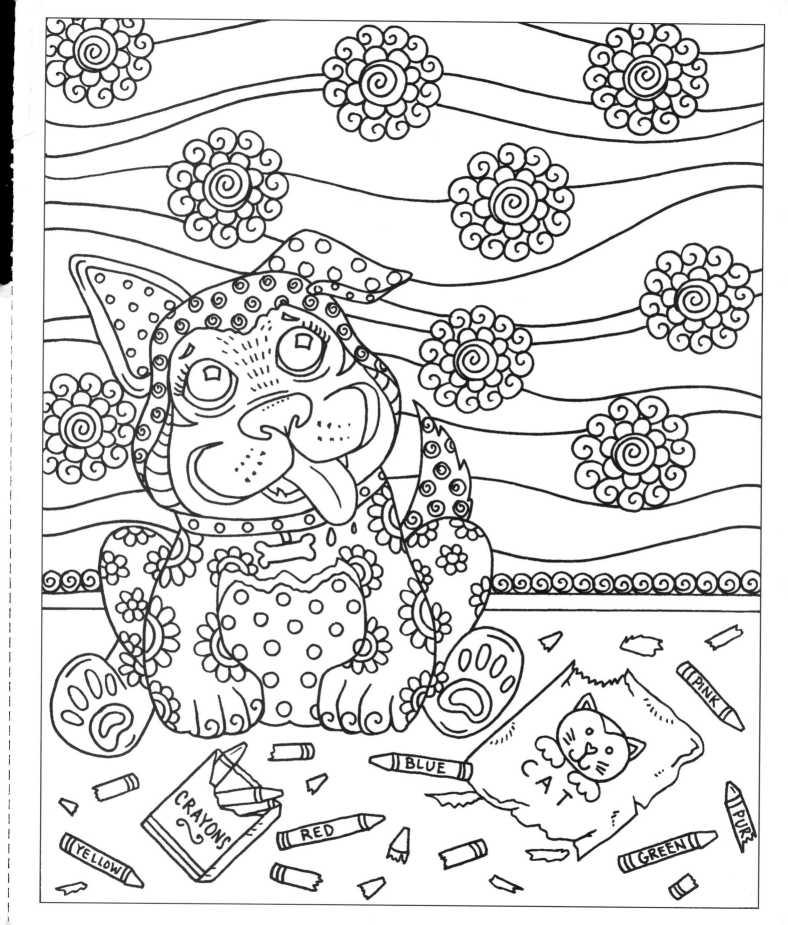